WHEN THE
SIELING
COMES
CRASHING
DOWN

WHEN THE
SIELING
COMES
CRASHING
DOWN

DR. KEVIN SIELING

XULON PRESS

Xulon Press
2301 Lucien Way #415
Maitland, FL 32751
407.339.4217
www.xulonpress.com

Unless otherwise indicated, The New Testament in Modern
English by J.B Phillips copyright © 1960, 1972 J. B. Phillips.
Administered by The Archbishops' Council of the Church of
England. Used by Permission.

Printed in the United States of America

Paperback ISBN-13: 978-0-5787-6610-2
Ebook ISBN-13: 978-1-6322-1845-2

DEDICATION

To all the members of my stand-up family who have lived these chapters of our story. I am forever in your gratitude for repeatedly picking yourselves up and shaking yourselves off even when this world tried to make you think, you are a little off-kilter. Trust me; you are not!

CONTENTS

Acknowledgments

I am indebted to everyone who encouraged and supported me throughout this remarkable season, as God put person, after person, after person in my path so I could check this venture off my bucket list.

A BIG thank you to the lunch bunch at SCA, who started it all because they kept saying, Doc you should write a book.

FOREWARD

Our family surname is of German descent and pronounced sē-liŋ or ceil·ing. This family moniker has provided others with several run of the mill jokes over the years. When your last name is associated with the overhead area of any room, inevitably, second rate jokes arrived in abundance. "What's holding you up, Sieling?", "Oh, so you think you are above us?" or "Look, I can touch the ceiling and never leave the ground." Unfortunately, a lot of lame cracks came with our last name.

Nevertheless, this book did not grow out of a necessity to decipher my heritage, but an idea that started as a small ember burning inside me; a deep yearning to tell our family story. With each whirlwind, our narratives were fanned until a flame grew bright and bold. That powerful flame symbolizes our deep-rooted faith. An unwavering belief that has served us well to build a firm foundation. A groundwork that kept us secure, steady, and upright when the winds of change or everyday chaos rocked the Sieling boats.

As our stories unfold, you will see I am just a guy from rural Minnesota, who did not want to repeat a cycle of abuse. I ridiculously thought that, if I did not have any children, I could somehow prevent the sins of my father.

In the first two chapters, you will learn more about me and the choices I made while searching for some meaning within a large family. Secretly, I was seeking some acknowledgment from my dad. In the end, I finally accepted my efforts would never, ever be good enough.

Chapter 3 is told by the woman with the generous heart I fell in love with. She reminds me often; I was clueless when she started courting me.

The goal of chapter 4 is to introduce you to my many siblings. Thanks to a 1986 article written by Bob Lind, a columnist for the Fargo Forum, you will meet the rest of "The Sieling Family."

In chapters 5, 6, and 7, you will come to know our biological children: Miranda, Evan, and Abby. Each has experienced some season of injustice but has come out of their tumultuous time a better person.

Chapters 8, 9, 10, and 11 introduces you to the four children we adopted: Stephanie, Edward, Harley, and Howard. Fostering and then moving forward with adoption is a lifelong commitment that often comes with life-changing events.

How does one even begin to comprehend a group of doctors' alerting you that Stephanie's diagnosis of fetal alcohol syndrome is so severe, it mirrors Alzheimer's? There are no words, only tears.

He couldn't always justify the cause, but I was aware of how anger looked on my father's face. After learning how a drug user's neglect disfigured a six-year-old boy, it was less problematic to rationalize Harley's bouts of rage. Each of their stories still inspires me.

Finally, in Chapter 12, I relate the saga of our first grandson whose repetitive actions landed him in a mental health facility. During that journey, his mom and dad joined the ranks of many parents, like us, who fought to overcome our fear of helplessness.

Without any doubt, my family has weathered their share of personal storms. This is our family story; their narratives are my legacy. I look forward to sharing our chapters with you.

I

NOT MY PATH

Growing up in the 1960s and '70s in rural Minnesota, was a simpler way of living compared to what awaited me as a future husband, father, and grandfather. I grew up on a small dairy farm between two rival towns. Our homestead was surrounded by vast meadows of prairie grass, grain fields of wheat and oats, groves of mature elm, maple, and oak trees, as well as shallow lakes and sloughs framed with waving cattails. A daily adventure was always 100% guaranteed when you lived in a three-bedroom house with your parents and ten biological siblings. Yes, that is right, ten siblings: seven boys and three girls.

My dad, Fred, was born in the summer of 1926 near the city of Perham, located in the heart of Minnesota's lake country along U.S. Highway 10. He was the son of a farmer; so naturally, farming became his way of life, and he would introduce his world to my beautiful mother. Marilyn Swanstrom, born in the winter of 1925, was a "townie" and Concordia College graduate.

After they married in 1947, they farmed near Perham until they moved to a dairy farm near Lake Park and Audubon; the place I have always called home. There, my Mom taught Home

1

Economics, and Dad made his living as a farmer, a grain elevator worker, and later, a real estate agent, and an income tax consultant. Labored with ten kids in twelve years, my Mom decided to stay at home serving as a full-time mother and a defender of children.

I believe my father's parents were both of German descent. My ancestral understandings led me to believe he was well-schooled in their cultural principles on strict parenting. Basically, my father was raised by no-nonsense parents. If my dad demonstrated a weakness of any kind, this inconvenience would be his problem. Excessive tenderness would have been a luxury, merely frivolous. Some stories suggest such a demeaning parenting style could explain away or excuse his actions. What I feared, as an offspring of this ethnic union, was that Fred would pass on his turbulent experiences to successive generations.

I can vividly recall this memory like it happened yesterday. I was sitting at a general Psychology class in Reed Hall in the spring of 1977. My professor was lecturing about a list of characteristics for a column labeled: "A Healthy, Stable Family." Then, he drew a thick, white line down the middle of the chalkboard and wrote one word at the top of the list: "Dysfunctional." On this side of the chart, as he wrote, he spoke the printed words aloud: physical abuse; verbal abuse; dominant controlling males; fear, and incest. I remembered squirming in my seat. By the end of the class, I was uncomfortable and feeling nauseous. My professor had just described my entire childhood and coined it all: dysfunctional. What was frightening me personally to the core—more than a column of words—my professor informed the class that when left unreported, these traits and actions can be passed down from generation to generation.

Memories from long ago lightly fade over time. Even so, what I had witnessed as an adolescent has never diminished. I was keenly aware that this cycle of dysfunction was bulldozing through my life.

To this day, I cannot remember a single holiday or large family gathering that did not end without my devoted Mother in tears. These tears—mostly a result of melancholy, fatigue, or despair—came after spending most of the morning planning and preparing a smorgasbord of food for a table for twenty; when my Dad would almost always find fault in her execution. Perhaps, he thought the preparation took too long, the cost of food was too high, there wasn't the right seating arrangement, the crust on one of the pies was too dark, or she had not basted the turkey enough. It did not matter; my Dad would always find a flaw in whatever my Mom had tried to accomplish. He would relentlessly belabor his point until tears rolled down her cheeks, continuing to badger her right up to the second the family or guests would arrive. Then Mom would quickly and quietly try to compose herself.

I had witnessed this so many times, that in my first week of marriage, when my new bride placed a plate of mashed potatoes with lumpy hamburger gravy in front of me, I hissed without missing a beat, "I can't eat this shit!" With slumped shoulders, my new wife took the plate from the table and dropped it loudly in the sink, food, and all. Without a single word but a discernable sniffle, she left the room. My first thought was not, "I win", or "I am the head of THIS house." No, I could see my bride was devastated; I had genuinely offended her. I sat there in silence. I could not allow DNA or my past to dictate my behavior. I did not, and could not, break her spirit. When I saw how my selfishness had hurt the heart of the woman I loved, my offensive words pierced me. On that day, I vowed I would never become my father.

With this in mind, it would be more accurate to say that I was on the same journey as the women in my family, as far as my career was concerned. My selfless mother and my great aunt were both teachers. I was influenced by these educators, even though I do not think I ever saw my mother teach. I knew she was a Home Economics teacher in the town of Audubon, but I attended school in neighboring Lake Park. After I started Kindergarten there, I was mesmerized by how teachers acted. I studied how they would change the volume of their voices, and the motion of their hands as they directed the rows of students in the hallways or lines for the buses. I was fascinated with how they knew everything about herbivores, carnivores, hexagons, pentagons, weather, food pyramids, early settlements, customs, or government. Teachers knew everything! Most of them reminded me of my loving mother; kind in temperament, offering some sweet, soothing words, or accepting a single, spontaneous hug without hesitation.

All through my elementary years, I have fond memories of acting out what I had often witnessed in my classrooms. I would imitate how I saw my teachers at school in the basement of our farmhouse. By the time I was in middle school, I had volunteered to be a teacher's assistant instead of taking a study hall. In high school, I became a member of a club that explored the teaching profession, and it offered students practical opportunities in real-time classrooms. So, it was not a stretch for me, upon my high school graduation, to pursue a career choice of an elementary teacher. Since then, I have been in the world of education. For over 40 years, I have been a teacher, academic dean, principal, head of school, director, and an educational consultant.

Now that I think of it, I do need to take that back. I did see my Mom teach one time. She had returned to education after my older siblings had graduated, but three of us were left at home and still attending high school. Mom was subbing at our school in Lake Park for Mr. McMahon, my U.S. History teacher. It was in the late spring of 1976; most of my classmates had come down with the common affliction known as senioritis. A trio of the guys was goofing around in the back of the room, near a moving bookcase presenting a barrier that separated two classrooms. This band of know-it-alls wasn't listening to a word my mother said, and there was no way I was going to try to defend her. As my mother moved about the room, I had not yet noticed a stack of books and a set of rolled-up maps precariously perched on the top of the rolling bookcase.

What I did notice, was my Mom making her way back to the corner of the room, where the troublemakers continued to banter back and forth, ignoring her efforts to teach the lesson. As she stood over them, my mother leaned in, placing her hand ever so slightly on the bookcase, advising the boys in a pleasant but stern voice I knew so well, "I need you three to stop talking and pay attention." With sly smirks, they responded, "Yes, Mrs. Sieling." Then, I saw her give the tiniest shove on the bookcase as she walked away. Suddenly, the maps and books came crashing down around the bewildered boys. Everyone looked in their direction, and the room abruptly went quiet. My wise mother turned back and stated, "Oh my, I hope you're okay," and without missing a beat she added, "I guess you weren't paying attention to that either." The red-faced trio didn't speak another word for the rest of the class period. I never talked about this incident with my Mom. I did not need her to affirm what I had already suspected. After raising ten kids, a U.S. History class with a trio of disrespectful boys was not her first rodeo; she knew exactly how to get their attention. After all, she was a teacher; she knew everything!

I believe my sweet, attentive but silent mother was determined to keep her definition of a family together, so she stayed strong for us kids and endured the abuse. In the '70s, women did not have the influential voices they do now, nor the vibrato to point out mistreatment, alerting the appropriate people to believe you, to support you or protect you. Later in life, I saw the same fortitude in my second daughter, as she fought to keep her description of a family together against the adversities of alcoholism, drugs, and infidelity. When we decided to adopt a 16-year-old who came from a world of drugs, abuse, and neglect; we reiterated to him, "Your past does not define you. The choices that you make, speaking honesty, being a man of your word, is what defines you and your character." This virtue, I learned from my mother, the teacher. I came to understand; it is your actions that define you. The same fortitude, I saw her endure for years.

I was determined to not repeat a sequence of destructive behaviors. My father's path would not be my path. I made a purposeful choice to follow in my mother's footsteps. I became the father of seven, a foster dad to over 25 kids, as well as a reliable and unwavering defender of children.

2

SEVENTH SON

What's My Number?

Can you remember the exact moment in your life when you knew, with complete certainty, the role you would play within your own family? Do you see yourself as the ultimate decision-maker, the wise peacemaker, judge and jury, the tender-hearted caretaker, the hometown hero, or the family scapegoat? Or, do you see yourself as the last, best piece of an intricate family puzzle? No matter the placement, first child, middle child, or any number in between, you fit perfectly. For one defining moment, you understand your position, your role, and your purpose in life. For most, such assurance would be received and welcomed. Unfortunately, for years, I never felt any of those certainties. It never happened. My quest continued for decades. What was my purpose? Where did I fit in? What exactly was my number?

Early on, a lack of confidence and a half-hearted process of elimination left me with only one solid answer: I was simply a placeholder in a string of ten kids. I realized I was number eight, but I hoped there would be something special about being the seventh son of seven boys. At the beginning of this journey, my number eight in the clan often was my placeholder. It was all I had.

Before I even became a twinkle in my dad's eye, first there was Diane. She was oldest of the ten. I am not sure how my dad felt about his first child being a girl. My guess is, my mom—an only child—was elated that her firstborn was a daughter. Yet, Dad and Mom made up for it quickly. Their next seven kids were all boys: Ron, Glen, Bruce, John, Larry, Dale, and then me. The next two; Connie, then Karen, both girls, were encouraged by my oldest sibling. Diane kept begging for a little sister. But, by the time the two girls came along, Diane was a preteen and already making her own way in a world of men. Through the years, Diane developed a close relationship with her sister siblings after Connie and Karen started families of their own.

Because my younger sisters and my older brother Dale, were closest to my age, I remember more shared happenings with each of them growing up. I simply inched up year after year, seemingly unnoticed, wanting to be closer to the same height and build as my more athletic brothers, but I knew it was unlikely. I yearned for any opportunity to be recognized or appreciated by the head of the tribe; my father. Inwardly, I knew, I would not be following in the footsteps of my brothers' well-worn cleats and basketball shoes. If food is the way to a man's heart, then sports was the fastest path to my father's soul. So, if you did not watch professional sports or play sports, your chances were slim to none you would ever make a connection with him.

Plus, seeing my older siblings mature and develop their mechanical skills and God-given talents, gave me little insight into my own future purpose. I remained troubled; searching for some significance in my role within a large family and acknowledgment from my dad. I revisited the idea that I somehow had to be more than an integer within an expanding tribe. Yet, little of what I did filled that void, but I kept circling back to that number. . . seven.

I think. I tried to force the number seven to be more noteworthy. In no way did it make sense. I never believed seven was lucky. I never used it as a guide to gamble in Vegas or use it as a final pick in a lottery ticket purchase. Maybe, because I was born on August 7th, I thought my digit should be more distinct. I clung to the notion that something had to be significant. After all, I was the seventh son, born on the 7th. According to some Bible scholars, the number seven means completeness.

I cannot explain why I needed a number, but I was aware I never wanted a big family. A large family was never my plan. I have always believed that my God has a spirited sense of humor. As part of His plan, He aligned my journey in such a way that, some sixty years later, I have been blessed with seven children of my own, and seven grandkids, thereafter. Each of them completes me, and gives me, purpose. As it turned out, with no foresight on my part, seven has actually become my lucky number.

Duck, Duck, Goose

If you grew up on a farm as I did, you might remember this phenomenon: there was always an abundance of animals. For our tribe, sustaining a small dairy farm meant lots of cows, a horse, some dogs, several cats, and flocks and flocks of chickens, ducks, and geese. I understood the cows and the chickens, but I could not see the need for geese and ducks. I would not ask my dad, mainly because I did not want to poke the bear. I believe that he just wanted these animals, so that became the status quo. We were all required to do chores, so a gaggle of domestic geese, like the all-white Embden were easy to care for. As far as fowl go, they were easily forgettable. Unless you needed a cooked goose for a seasonal family gathering.

I did not understand, nor did I probe why my father went to the trouble of digging a deep trench near the slough, filling it with water, then surrounding the area with fencing; all to provide an enclosure for these geese. Perhaps he was determined to earn some local bragging rights when he added a small group of Canadian honkers to the flock. You couldn't argue, they were majestic birds; their markings were so distinct. This gaggle truly stood out against the plain white birds sharing the enclosure. A few times each year, we would help my dad corner the birds and capture them, holding them firmly on the ground while he clipped one set of their wings. He assured us that this would keep the birds off balance so they could never fly away. The Canadian and the Embden were both a strong breed, each could easily adjust to the sub-zero temperatures of Minnesota if they were left outside. However, with the first snow of the season, we would herd them into the barn to help them settle in for the long winter.

Somehow, on a bitterly cold winter night, a group of six snow-white Embden left their sanctuary and escaped their indoor coop. I do not recall who was responsible for accidently allowing it to happen, but it did not matter. The deed was done. On that fateful evening, one of my older brothers arrived home and innocently left his car parked in our driveway. No one knew it at the time, as the heavy snow was falling, but these crazy birds squeezed under the frame of his car and huddled under the engine for warmth. When my brother returned to his vehicle, to merely pull his car closer to the garage and plug-in the engine heater, there was no time for the ill-fated flock to escape. All six geese were crushed under the moving car; not one of the wayward fowl would survive.

My first recollection of the night began when I heard my dad browbeating one of my brothers as he stomped down the stairs, each carrying a clump of limp geese, less their long necks and heads. With the rest of the boy's barracks fully awake, we stood together, no one talking. All I heard were some nervous feet shuffling back and forth near the stove in the kitchen upstairs. Then, I saw one of my brothers using mom's big oven mitts, carrying a large canning pot of water down the steps. I could see the steam rising off the surface of the water as he placed the pot on the cement floor next to the pile of birds. Then one by one, my dad would dip a blood-soaked carcass into scalding hot water to loosen the matted feathers. As soon as he pulled them out, he threw the wet steaming mass at our feet and ordered us to start plucking. It did not matter that most of us had been asleep for hours before the incident; if someone had made a mistake then we all had to pay. If any of us grumbled about the time or the task, the guilty brother might receive another hard smack across the back of his head. Worse, we could each get a whack for complaining. When the task was done, he had made his message clear. Our lesson for the night was over. Dad dropped the geese in the freezer and without a word between us, we all went back to bed.

A Burning Question

Similar life lessons from my father were infamously quick, yet often painful. On many occasions, he found these lessons were best executed in groups. I want to believe his primary objective was to ensure, history (or what he deemed as mistakes) would never be repeated. To conduct a group lesson was deliberately more efficient on his part. Think about it, he basically had a classroom of ten students at his fingertips. My father gave the impression his teachings, in the presence of your siblings, would prove to be more meaningful and memorable for you. In our frazzled minds, we often found comfort in being physically near each other, as we each took our turn as he delivered the punishment with his belt or the leather strap. I came to despise his group approach. This method was nothing more than a form of intimidation. The incidents were humiliating, and you could never predict the intensity of the reprimand. The consequence never felt logical. I witnessed more than once an older brother receiving a sharp blow to the face for his alleged offense. I think we were always presumed guilty by association, never innocent. This was the burning question rattling around in my brain. Why did we often receive the same number of blows, even if we were not the primary offender?

My big lesson began innocently enough. There was a dense grove of trees that surrounded the farmhouse. This was a great place to explore and build forts; a superior spot to just be kids. In one open area of the grove, my younger sisters and I had assembled a collection of old wooden chairs and other broken pieces of furniture. One of our prized pieces was an old wood stove, discarded from a dilapidated fish house. This lovely little location with our collection of relics became a safe haven for hours and hours of imaginative play. Not far from our makeshift fort, was the chicken coop. Each morning we would collect the eggs for the day and bring them to the house. One day, my two sisters and I, had the grand idea of keeping a few eggs for ourselves. We built a small fire in the old wood stove and fried up the eggs as a little treat. After we had sampled the fried eggs, we put out the fire in the old stove and continued with our carefree day.

I am not sure who reported our adventure in the woods, but at first, I was not certain why Dad called me and my two sisters into the kitchen. As he began to deliver his detection of our adventure with the stove, I could feel the sweat forming on the back of my neck. Frying eggs in the woods was not innocent to him. He was explaining the dangers of recklessness, recalling the tragic house fire of years before my time, and what happened if fire got out of control. Since none of that happened, I was hoping the stern lecture was enough. I was sadly mistaken.

He told me to put both my hands in front of me and hold them straight out. Next, he grabbed the box of stick matches and struck one against the side of the box, and lit a candle. He pulled my hand forward and held the candle inches away from my outstretched fingers. I was reminded of the pain from accidentally touching a hot pot on the stove or a cup of recently brewed coffee. In each of those cases, I quickly jerked my hand away from the source of heat. This feeling growing deep inside me was immensely different as my dad held a tight grip on my hand. I could not move it up or down or side to side. I could not take my eyes off the flame as he moved it closer and closer to my extended fingers. The searing pain was immediate and intense. The heat from the flame was penetrating because I could not move away from the source. The strain of the moment made me want to pass out. I could feel big salty tears rolling down my cheeks. I bit down hard on my lower lip to prevent me from saying anything. I did not want to cry out for fear that he would move to my other hand. My fingers, now weaker from his tight grip, started to tremble. I could see the motion of my shaking hand make the flame flicker. Even though I could not see my fingertips, they felt tender and were growing bright crimson like my cheeks. Then without warning, he stopped, the incident and lesson were over. His actions left their intended mark. I never played with matches or fire again. Nonetheless, I never forgot or forgave him for this lesson he carried out in front of my impressionable little sisters. As the older brother, the one who should have known better, I took the heat in order to spare them a similar life lesson.

I could not always spare my sisters from my dad. Interestingly enough, as adults, my sisters cannot agree on the details, but I recall their stories of his inappropriate touching when they were getting ready for bed and tales of dad in their room long after they tried to sleep. One of the most traumatic incidents ended with my younger sister accusing my dad of unwanted advances. He was trying to brush it off by telling my mom she was overreacting. When my mom tried to stand up to him and protect her daughters, my dad hit her. Something inside me boiled to the top and I jumped on my dad's back trying to prevent him from hitting her again. As we spun in circles, I could see my mom reaching for a frying pan out of the corner of my eye. I think she was planning to use it on my dad. He must have seen it too, because he reached his hand over his shoulder, yanking me by the hair and pulling me off. Sending me sliding across the floor into my mother's advancing steps. Afterward, for a few minutes, there was nothing but silence, only the heavy breathing from each of us standing motionless in the kitchen.

As I said before, even though I have tried to have conversations with my sisters about my father, they could never agree on what really happened behind closed doors. I believe something occurred because years later, one of my brothers was accused of similar inappropriate actions with his own daughter. I find it hard to imagine that parallel actions simply occur in isolation. The sad part about family secrets, whether or not they are witnessed by others or if they are only spoken with whispered breaths, the acts are not imagined; the victims know what actually occurred. For me, the news of my brother's allegations opened a floodgate of repressed memories that eventually paralyzed me. I started suffering from severe panic attacks, crippling me mentally and physically. I experienced crushing chest pain, vertigo, lightheadedness, and feelings I would die at any minute. The physical symptoms wore me down mentally. I had to take a leave of absence from my job. For more than nine months, I was a wreck. Through intensive personal therapy, I was able to come back and function enough to work part-time, but the memories of abuse haunted me for years.

What do children do, who live with a parent, whose mood flips like a light switch, and you are always uneasy in his presence? You learn to adapt. You become an expert at avoidance.

You find places where you can evade or escape the tormentor. Luckily, a farm is vast enough to avoid detection. For me, I found mundane individualized chores like mowing grass and gardening to be soothing. In the planting phase, it could still be tense, but eventually calm and comfort came around. At first, I had to endure the watchful eye of my father. I had to prove I could hoe straight rows, with furrows the exact depth, to accept the seeds one at a time. You must shake the packages ever so slightly, just enough to not waste them in the first few inches of the assigned row. With practice and permission, I would be allowed to cover each channel with a mixture of freshly turned soil and cow manure.

Next, came endless stretches of watering until those delightful days when tiny green sprouts came shooting through the black blanket of topsoil. You could stroll through the garden looking at ribbons of wavy green lettuce, shoots of silky lattice fern-like carrot tops, and the triangular fuzzy leaves of cucumbers. From the tendrils of pea plants to the strong stalks of sweet corn, and pumpkins, it was all worth it under his watchful eye. Maintaining the lawn and garden turned out to be my passion in my teens. During the annual grain harvest, to see my mother prepare a spread of ripe tomatoes, steamed sweet corn, sliced cucumbers, mounds of mashed potatoes, and buttered green beans helped me discover and define part of my journey as a contributor. Growing an abundance of vegetables for the family table, pickled, or preserved in mason jars in the basement pantry, all provided me with a private feeling of acceptance and accomplishment.

Gardening proved to be purposeful, but it could not turn into a paying job. As soon as I took my written test to earn my farmers' permit, I was out looking for part-time employment. Somehow, I landed an interesting job working at Fort Detroit, a tourist attraction and deer park, west of Detroit Lakes, Minnesota. Who gets to say they were offered the chance to ride shotgun for an actual working stagecoach? I got to say that. It was my first paying job and I genuinely enjoyed the uniqueness of it. I would take their prepaid tickets, help the riders on and off the coach, and then sit next to the driver as we meandered through the trail within the deer park. The driver and I repeated the route over and over throughout the summer. With the approach of my senior year in high school, this seasonal job was over, but for a guy's first paycheck, it was memorable.

My Time

It was 1976. I felt my final year of high school would be my time to finally prove to my father I had some worth in specific areas like academics. For me, strong academics could possibly pay off monetarily and provide me with a direct path to college. I purposely positioned myself to be the first of the ten-sibling tribe to attend a four-year university. I had studied hard, took higher-level classes, and my grades were exceptional. If all went the way I had projected, I would finish in one of the top two academic positions, if not class valedictorian. I was an active member of 4-H, participated in their radio speaking contest, and the annual Share-The Fun Talent show. I earned first place in each of these events. I had been in declamation or speech all through high school and earned different awards. This was going to be my year. This was my last chance to earn a coveted title. I chose an emotional monologue of a tormented Judas Iscariot grasping the fact he had betrayed Christ for a meager thirty pieces of silver. I received highest honors at district, region, and finally captured one of the top ten desired spots in the state in the category of Serious Drama. I did not earn first or second, settling for 4th in the state, but brought home a shiny medallion to prove it. I rounded out the school year with my peers selecting me to speak at our graduation and published my first piece of writing with the class prophecy for the 76' Parker yearbook. Each of these accomplishments was noticed in my college application and acceptance to Moorhead State University. With the numerous scholarships and grants, I received, along with a guaranteed work-study subsidiary, my cost to attend college would be minimal for my parents. Financially, I could afford to go to school. To ensure I would have more than enough funds, I started looking for another job, away from the farmstead.

One morning, I started my voluntold list of chores by using our gas-powered rototiller, to break up the soil and churn over the weeds filling the areas between the rows of vegetables in the garden. Each year we added more space to the garden plot, so it took most of the morning to finish. To clearly see rich, dark rows between plush green plants with an abundant crop ready to peak was always satisfying. Then, I used both a push mover and the riding lawnmower to cut the grass around the house and the expansive side yards near the county and granary roads. Earlier in the week, a pile of rock had been deposited in the front yard and Dad wanted it all moved and spread out to cover the areas of the front yard where grass no longer grew. By late afternoon, with the gardening and mowing done, I had not started on the rock. When I went inside to get a cool drink, I dropped down on the couch to rest for a few minutes and must have fallen asleep. The next thing I remember, I was seeing stars. I mean, literally with my eyes still closed, I was seeing stars. Oddly, I was also feeling pain. Did bright stars cause pain? As I opened my eyes, I realized I was being punched in the face, repeatedly. I lifted my arms and hands to protect my face, rolling off the couch onto the floor. Then, I felt the first kick to my ribs. It took my breath away; there was so much discomfort. Somehow, I was able to stumble to my feet. At the same moment, I stood upright and identified my assailant. It was my father.

My ears were ringing from the blows to my face. I was not clear-headed, but I was able to see his mouth moving. As his sounds and words began to intensify, I saw a face filled with anger. He was shouting at me, "I only asked you to do one thing! One damn thing! You can't even do that! Instead, I find your lazy ass sleeping on the couch! You are sound asleep! I can't believe it!" Then he was pushing me from the back towards the front door. As I opened the screen door to step out onto the landing, I felt a hard kick to my lower backside. With nothing in front of me, I lost my footing and I tumbled down the cement steps. I landed with a thud on the hard cement pad. As I rolled over, I looked up at my father's scarlet face. I could see nothing but contempt in his eyes. He looked down on me, and spits out, "You are such a piece of shit! You are a worthless piece of shit! If I had a gun right now, I would shoot you."

I will always remember my father in this moment. There was nothing, absolutely nothing I could ever do to please this man. After taking years of physical and verbal abuse, I understood my efforts would never, ever be good enough. I started on my hands and knees, then rose using my knees. I was on both feet, facing him. As I looked up towards the house, I had dropped my shoulders in resolve. I inhaled deeply and started walking towards him, slowly making my way up the steps, one at a time. As I got to the top step, we made eye contact. My dad sputtered, "Where the hell do you think you are going?" I stared into his eyes of disdain, "I am going to get you the gun."

As he raised his hand, I reacted instinctively by turning my face away to avoid another direct hit. Instead, to stop me, he uneasily placed his hand on my chest. "Just stop. Why do you make me do that? Why can't you just do what I ask you to do?"

As my father had done so many times in my past, his teaching time was over. He turned around, stepped inside, and closed the door behind him. I just stood there on the cement steps, holding my tender side where the ache from his forceful kicks and blows started flooding my brain. Through the throbbing pain, an idea started to grow. The hell with looking for a job. I had to leave home. I could no longer live here.

By the end of the week, only mutterings had been exchanged between my father and me. With no paternal apology looming, I placed a call to Moorhead State University. My college advisor informed me that since I had already been accepted, I could take three of my core freshmen classes during the two summer sessions. In fact, I could earn a total of 18-credits for a solid head start; a fresh start. I could move into the dorm by the end of the week and leave this life behind me. I jumped at this unexpected opportunity. In the late spring of our nation's bicentennial, ten days after I graduated from high school, I started my freshman year at MSU. Unpredictably, the Parker graduation motto, the one I had helped select as a senior class officer, turned out to be ever so fitting, "*We had grown up together, to go out alone.*"

3

ROOF FINDS A FUTURE WIFE

Christened, Debra Renee Runkle, I was born May 10, 1957. I grew up in Stewartville, a bedroom community, six miles from Rochester, Minnesota, the home of IBM and the Mayo Clinic. I had three older brothers. As the youngest of four and only girl, you might think my parents would want to spoil me, but that could not have been farther from the truth. Instead, my purpose-driven parents showed me the importance of working hard and serving where the Lord called you to do so. My dad, Ken, was a maintenance guy at IBM and handyman of all sorts in our quiet town in southern Minnesota. As our family provider, my Dad felt he was blessed and gratefully gave back. My Mom, Maxine, never worked outside the home. She was a genuine domestic engineer.

Gathering from my Sunday school lessons, I concluded my parents were good, Christian people. When Mom died in the summer of 2019, I was proudly reminded by her pastor that my Mother lived fully by the Book. She was a devout Christian and a fervent believer of God's Word. Pastor Fritz informed those who attended her funeral, he remembered my parents coming to church every Saturday or Thursday night. From the time he started in 2001, my parents would arrive at the church a half-hour before he or anyone else. They would open the doors, turn on all the lights and wait in the Narthex to greet their fellow parishioners. They obediently demonstrated the role of faithful stewards and I was certain they walked with God every day. They read *Our Daily Bread* devotional and family Bible without fail. My parents routinely sat at the kitchen table, witnessing in full view of my siblings, as well as visiting childhood friends. Mom or Dad would take turns, finishing their nightly Bible study before turning in for the evening. They did not falter; my parents' faith was constant.

When I was sixteen, a sophomore, my parents had their faith tested beyond measure. My brother Gary, a senior at Stewartville High School was driving under a bridge on a frigid February evening and according to the authorities, he hit a patch of black ice, spun out of control, and flipped his vehicle. He was crushed by the weight of the car and died at the scene. I do not remember much about the accident; I think I was in shock for the next few months of my life. I rarely discussed the details with my Mother, I could sense it was too painful for her to talk about. What I do remember is when the pastor of our church came to our house and told my parents the unexpected, heartbreaking news. Then over the next few days, hundreds of people came through our home; I do mean hundreds of people bringing an onslaught of hotdishes and their condolences. What I did not realize until much later was that out of such painful tragedy, something amazing would happen.

I graduated from the same high school that my brother attended in May of 1975. With only a week off, I started the June session of a clerical program at Rochester Vocational Institute. It was a ten-month course of study and I received my clerical certificate by March. With credentials in hand, I decided to move to Florida. The boy I liked and dated in high school had relocated to Florida and I followed him there. I quickly got an office job at Kmart ready to start the next chapter of my life, but this only lasted a few months. This boy

I liked, who I thought liked me, ended our relationship soon after my arrival. By October, I packed up my belongings along with a better understanding of what I wanted in future relationships and moved back home to Minnesota.

I had grown fond of my new-found independence; so, I knew I had to provide for myself and find a different job right away. My career in banking started with First National in Stewartville, and I moved into an apartment in Rochester with my high school classmates and forever friends, Judy, and Pam. I kept working at the bank until I decided to attend Moorhead State University in September of 1977. I had done some research and read that Moorhead State, in northern Minnesota, had a reputable Social Work program. I cannot pinpoint one thing that called to me to this profession, but perhaps it was the untimely death of my brother. Something in me was yearning for a career where I would be helping people.

On my first day at Moorhead State University, my new roommate walked into our dorm room and we started to make conversation. I wanted to get to know her better, so I suggested we go buy a bottle of Boone's Farm Strawberry Hill, head to a local park, and just sit and chat. We spent the next three hours at Gooseberry Park talking about our lives, how she was worried about being stuck with a Freshman, and what brought each of us to Moorhead State. We found out that we were both transplants from other schools, now mutually enrolled in the same Social Work program. We learned that we were practically the same age, our birthdays were just one day apart. In three short hours, we solidified what would become a 40-year friendship.

In February, someone in our dorm came back from class stating that one of the guys from across the hall, had a brother who had died unexpectedly. They thought his name was "Roof." Later, I learned his name was Kevin. Since my brother had died similarly without warning, I found out where Kevin's room was and went over to find him. His door was open, so I knocked on the frame and introduced myself. I never thought I would use the tragedy of my brother's death as an opener for an introduction. My conversation was mostly one-sided. I just wanted him to know that if he ever needed to talk, I could listen. I finished with, "If you just need a friend, a shoulder to cry on, I can do that. I've been through the same thing." Kevin or "Roof" thanked me, then told me his brother, who was only two years older and a healthy father of two, went into the hospital for a routine appendectomy and never came home. We did not talk again that week, but we began a conversation that has spanned over 40 years.

Roof

The way Kevin tells the story, he was sitting in a co-ed lounge of Snarr Hall in September of 1977, when a tall but pudgy guy with thick black-rimmed glasses walked in, pointed at Kevin, and said, "What's your name?" He looked up at the guy towering over him and responded, "Kevin, Kevin Sieling." The big guy offered a funny smirk and countered, "Ceiling, like Roof?" Kevin answered, "Sure" and that became his Snarr Hall moniker for the next three years. Kevin told me later that he liked his new nickname, "I was starting a new journey, and I had a new name to go with it. I would now be known as Roof." He thought the name was fitting.

Overcoming Pillars

A favorite college hangout for our dorm mates that year was Trader and Trapper. Every Friday night, there were crackers and crocks of cheese spread upstairs, and disco dancing with 25-cent pitchers of beer downstairs. The Snarr crew rarely missed a Friday night to unwind; from what I witnessed, Kevin liked to dance for hours under that big spinning silver ball. Close to the end of the year, the crew wanted to celebrate an evening visiting all our usual hangouts in down-town Moorhead: Mike's Office, Trader and Trapper, and the Lamplighter Lounge. Kevin thought it would be fun to ride a tandem bicycle to the local taverns. Kevin rarely drinks hard liquor when he is out, but for some reason, he was drinking a lot that evening. In fact, at one point in the night, I think he even slid under the table and passed out. After last call, Kevin, a little refreshed from his nap but still a little unsteady on his feet, insisted he could find his way back to the dorm.

He was searching for a riding partner and was incredibly determined to be the person steering the tandem bicycle. I thought this could be fun; we were not that far from campus, so I jumped on. We were riding along the sidewalks and I could see Snarr Hall a few feet away. Without warning, Kevin steered the bike into one of the pillars in front of the building. We hit the stone pillar with such force that we both flew forward off the bike, but landed in the only patch of grass near the bike rack. I remember standing up and yelling at Kevin, "That hurt you jerk! I think you involuntarily sterilized me! I better be able to have kids someday! If I can't, I am going to find you and cas-trate you!" I knew I was in pain, but what I did not know, was that I was shouting at my future husband, and thankfully, the future father of my three kids.

Kevin and I did not talk much after our crash, but I knew the Snarr crew would all be heading back to their respective homes for the summer. Kevin told us he was making plans to work at a gas station while saving up some money to travel to California to meet up with his brother who was being dis-charged from the Marines. He was hoping that he could con-vince his brother to move to Moorhead with him where the two of them could share an apartment near campus. I was headed back to Stewartville to work at the bank, but before I left, I asked Kevin for his summer address. I had every intention of writing to him so he would not forget me. I was delighted when Kevin wrote back a few times. I discovered he liked to write. Yet, I could tell by his meanderings that he did not have a clue I liked him. Kevin admitted to me later that he was clueless, he was recovering slowly from a bad breakup but was ready to start dating again.

When we both returned to Moorhead State in September, Kevin had traveled back from California and moved into an apartment with his brother. There was a 'Welcome Back to School' party that first weekend and all the Snarr girls wanted to go to another party. When I heard Kevin was hosting a small get together too, I informed the girls I was going to Kevin's party instead. I had my girlfriends drop me off at Kevin's new apartment in south Moorhead, and I stayed late into the night. That was when I met a member of Kevin's family for the first time: his brother, Dale. He was one year older than Kevin and was anxious to meet his younger sibling's friends. Dale was also hoping to meet and secure a date for his brother for a family event happening in a few weeks.

A few days later, I was pleasantly surprised when Kevin called to invite me to his parent's 35th wedding anniversary celebration. I learned later that Kevin had offered up the name of another girl at Moorhead State, but I had made a more favorable impression with Dale; as a result, he strongly suggested that Kevin invite me to their family event. I was happy that I had met Dale before the anniversary party. I tried to remember everyone else I met that evening and believe me, there were a lot of them when you figured in their parents, their siblings, their siblings' spouses, or significant others. I think their immediate family alone filled the main room but adding the aunts and uncles, friends, and neighbors, the hall was packed to capacity. I found I could relax around his family and I had a wonderful time at their celebration. Before we left to go back to campus, Kevin found me alone and we had our first kiss. In the months that followed the anniversary party, we spent every weekend together.

The Tank

As the cold Minnesota winter weather settled in, Kevin preferred to drive my 1959 four-door, full-sized, Pontiac Bonneville. It was maroon and white with several amenities that made it fun to drive: a good working radio, big rearview mirror, power brakes, a wraparound windshield, white side-wall tires, and these long tailfins. It was a solid, dependable car. My dad bought it for $500; he knew this vehicle would safely get me back and forth from Stewartville to Moorhead. Picture a tank or a snowplow, with wings.

One weekend, the guys and girls decided to drive to the Cormorant Pub for dinner. Kevin and I invited his younger sister and his sister-in-law to join us in the tank on the drive over. Located in Cormorant Village, a few miles from his parent's new lake home, the Cormorant Pub was a typical gathering place for his family because of the fun atmosphere and delicious homestyle cooking. The narrow road weaved through the trees and up and down a few steep hills as you made your way to the lakeshore entrance. As Kevin drove down one of the steep hills, he did not realize until it was too late, that the road was glare ice; the Pontiac started fishtailing. Efforts to counter-steer were futile as the car swiftly skated down the hill, left the road, and smashed into a big birch tree. The back-seat riders received most of the injuries, from bruises and scrapes on their shins to a bloody scratch on his little sister's nose.

After making sure everyone was okay, Kevin walked to the Pub and called his Dad to come pull the car out of the ditch. His dad came a few minutes later, assessed the damage, hooked up a chain, and pulled the Bonneville back onto the road. There was some damage to the grille, but we knew the tank was safe to drive. As we stood outside the Pub, waiting for Kevin to find us, I saw his dad standing in front of him with an entourage of brothers nearby. As I walked over, I heard Kevin's dad yelling at him, shouting, "How can you be so **stupid**! Only an **idiot** would drive that fast on an icy hill! You are such a **dumb shit**! Look, you even hurt your sister. I can't believe how **stupid** you are!"

My cheeks burned red, and without thinking, I stepped between Kevin and his father. As the words came out, I could hear my voice getting louder. I heard myself shouting, too. I hollered, "Kevin is the nicest person I've ever met. He would never hurt anyone on purpose. Fred, this was an accident!" I could see out of the corner of my eye; all of Kevin's brothers took two big steps back. I found out later, they all thought I was going to get punched by their dad. I did not. I am fairly sure I earned his respect that night because Fred never spoke to me in that tone again if Kevin and I were together. Kevin told me later, he had already decided to propose that night, but watching me defend him to Fred, sealed the deal. We got engaged that winter, barely weeks after we officially started dating.

Kevin's family planned a pre-wedding party for us at his Mom and Dad's lake home on Big Cormorant Lake in June of 1979. At one point in the afternoon, Fred pulled Kevin and me aside and brought us out to the garage where he pointed to a maple antique table and six cloth-covered, matching chairs. Fred told me that he typically spent $300 on each of his kids for a wedding gift. Since this table cost him close to $400, we only owed him $100. Once again, I took my stance facing Fred, this time in a much softer tone, I replied, "Thank you for thinking of us, but Fred, we don't have a hundred dollars to spend on a table. And it is not really a wedding gift if we have to pay for it." I left it at that. Later that night, Fred found me alone and told me that the table and chairs were ours, no strings attached.

That was how the relationship with my Father-in-law went up until he died in 2001. He never questioned me or challenged me. In reality, I never gave him another chance. That did not mean I'd ever let my guard down either. I was still cautious of his temperament around Marilyn. Throughout the years, I could not help but notice Kevin's Mom always managed to have new or healing bruises on her arms, wrists, or other visible areas. If I questioned her, Marilyn would counter, the marks came from Brandy, their hyperactive Irish Setter, or she had clumsily bumped into an open cupboard or dresser drawer. I had my theories; I had my doubts.

Kevin and I were at their lake house almost every weekend. Maintaining a protective eye on his Mom was the primary reason Kevin organized our numerous family stays on Big Cormorant Lake. Fishing, swimming, boating; their lake home had so much to offer for fun family gatherings. Looking ahead, Kevin insisted, if we had children, they would always sleep in the same bedroom as us, no matter what their ages. As their defender, Kevin promised he could not allow his children to sleep in a room separate from us if Fred was in the house. My husband vowed he would never, ever leave his children alone with his father. I understood why he had to draw this line in the sand that fall, we were expecting our first child in December of 1980

4

THE SIELING FAMILY – THEY HELP EACH OTHER TRAVEL LIFE'S BUMPY ROAD

The Forum: Sunday, January 5, 1986
By Bob Lind: Neighbor's Columnist

People drift in and out. Some sip hot cider. A young woman talks on the phone. Someone ties into a sandwich. Some sit down or stand around and talk. And someone – Marilyn, naturally – holds Chipper the dog on her lap. "That's the way it always is around here," Mary Sieling says. Mary found out about the Sieling family by marrying into it. She says her marriage to Ron Sieling paid a bonus. "You fall in love with the whole family, not just one person," she says. "They're always there."

There have been times when this close-knit family of 10 children headed by Fred and Marilyn Sieling could have come unraveled. But it didn't despite extremely trying times. Marilyn suffered a severe stroke. Fred has what he calls "a diabetic problem." A daughter had marital problems.

In 1978, a son, Larry, died and was buried the day before his son was born.

In 1986, Karen, the youngest child, died three weeks after her baby was born.

Besides that, Fred's brother-in-law died shortly after Larry's death and Marilyn's aunt died not long after Karen's death. Somehow, the family made it. "This family is special," son Kevin says. "This family can pull together when we need to."

The Sielings once farmed near Audubon, Minnesota. Fred and Marilyn lived in a house with a magnificent view of Big Cormorant Lake, about 8 miles south of Lake Park. Their children grew up: Diane, of Maine; Ron and Glen of Detroit Lakes; Bruce of Audubon; John of Detroit Lakes; Larry; Dale, in the service; Kevin of Rothsay, Minn.; Connie, a student at North Dakota State University; and Karen. "I'm an only child and I raised a crew like this?" Marilyn wonders.

Fred owns the Continental Land Co. in Detroit Lakes. Marilyn works as his secretary twice a week. "The rest of the time," Diane says, 'she stays home and takes care of grand-children, dogs, and everything else." Supporting one another is the name of the Sieling game. "If anyone needs anything, and I mean anyone, we're right there," Diane says. "There is a lot of love here. We're all very fortunate to have each other." While she was going through the misery of a divorce in Maine, "I was at a pretty low point." Diane says. "But then Terri (Larry's wife) came to Maine to help me. Then the family organized a 'telephone tree.' Each one had a day assigned to call to see if I was OK. I don't know what would have happened to me without them."

When they decided Diane needed to come home, Glen, Terri, and Karen's husband Richard Curtis made the 37-hour drive to get her. With the help of a rented trailer, two cars, two CBs, and lots of coffee, they brought Diane and her two children back to Minnesota. "I'm still tired," Richard says. "But it was worth it for the fresh lobster we had out there." Larry and

Terri had one son, Jeremy, and were expecting their second child when Larry, 21, had appendicitis surgery. He developed a blood clot a week later and died. Their son Tony was born the day after the funeral. Then, three weeks after Richard's wife Karen, 24, delivered their only child Andrew, she also developed a blood clot. Andrew was baptized one Sunday morning and Karen died that night.

Marilyn can't stop the tears as she thinks of it. Her son-in-law Richard pulls out some tissue. "I came prepared," he says. "Mom cries a lot," her daughter-in-law Mary says, "but I cry with her." Sometimes we all get going." Diane says. "The good Lord knows what's best," Fred says. "The main thing is to have faith and keep that faith. I don't know what people would do if they didn't have God to turn to." Then he points proudly to Andrew, now four months old. "What do you think of the little guy?" he asks. "He's pretty special."

My parents have 16 grandchildren," Kevin says, "and you'd think each one was the first one." Two more grandchildren are on the way. With the size of the family, having a crowd around is routine. They used to call the downstairs of their old farmhouse the "dormitory," because all the boys slept there. "They'd get into things," Marilyn says. "Once they started a fire under the gas barrel. I don't know why we didn't lose the whole house."

Fred made frequent use of a leather strap, particularly on the boys, Diane says. "I got their attention pretty easy," Fred grins. The family went through food like Sherman through Georgia. "We'd butcher two beefs," Fred says, "at about 1,000 pounds each, three hogs, about 175 chickens and have 2,200 pounds of potatoes. We'd go through that every year, plus fish and fowl. The seven boys seemed like they had hollow legs.

"We'd buy six or seven pairs of shoes at a time. They had lots of hand-me-downs, too." "Ron said he never had socks that matched," Mary says. "He got what was left." The boys slept three to a bed, and everyone had chores to do. "One good thing about having lots of brothers," Diane says, "is I didn't have to do the milking." "But when you get that many children and they all turn out good," Fred says, "that's quite an accomplishment. The in-laws, the ones the kids married, they're good, too."

"When I started going with Karen," Richard says, "I was kind of worried, because she said she had umpteen brothers and sisters, and I've only got one sister." No problem now, "I couldn't have married into a better family," he says. Both Dale and Kevin were married in 1979. That same summer, Bruce, and his girlfriend eloped. "I think they saw what the rest of us went through," Kevin says. Marilyn is doing all right since her stroke, she says, "but everyone thinks I've lost a little up here," and she taps her head. "We don't know if that's from the stroke or from raising 10 kids," Richard says.

Those 10 had wild nicknames when they were young – names like Snorkey, Ratso, Flubsie, Professor Poptop, and Loppy Lee. Kevin has been known as Roof since college, Sieling is pronounced "ceiling."

The family likes to gather at Mom and Dad's home in the summer, go out on the lake, play Trivial Pursuit and whist ("And chase kids." Diane says) and "eat lots of good food, which everyone contributes, so I don't get hit hard." Marilyn adds. There are special days, too, as when they have birthday parties for several at one time, or for one special person, such as Marilyn when she was 60 recently. "I'd have liked to stay in bed all day," she says, "but Fred invited all our old friends over, and had food ready. I told him I was going to get back at him someday."

Marilyn relaxes with a cup of coffee and with Chipper the dog on her knee. "Chip and mother are inseparable," Fred says. Happily, Brandy, the other dog, isn't on her lap. The Irish setter is so large that Diane wants to put antlers on him "because he's a moose," she says. The thought makes Marilyn Laugh. There are no tears now. "My folks don't dwell on what they can't have back," Kevin says. "For them, it's what they can do moving forward.

This article has been reprinted with permission from The Forum of Fargo-Moorhead.

5

SEASONS OF JOY

When Deb went into labor with our first baby, I did not know what to expect. Days earlier, my wife had given us a little scare when she slipped on an icy sidewalk while leaving her bank and landed hard on her stomach. Even after reassurances from Deb's doctor, I continued to worry. I worried throughout the pregnancy; I shamelessly fretted inwardly about being a dad. Deb's unexpected fall on the ice, so close to her due date, did not ease my mind in the least. As an expectant father, I was a mess. I experienced sympathetic morning sickness every day of Deb's first trimester. Even after we did all the prenatal visits, Lamaze breathing, and birthing classes; I was still totally unprepared for the big event.

First Daughter

Through all the doctor visits, we never asked to know the sex of our first baby. I did not want to add unnecessary gender worry to my growing list of "things to do". Nevertheless, after 24 hours of labor and some heavy-duty pushing, Miranda Joy Sieling, entered this world on December 14, 1980; looking more like one of the Coneheads from the planet Remulak on a Saturday Night Live skit. Secretly, I was praying for a girl; I was thrilled when our little Connie Conehead doppelgänger was finally placed in my arms.

We were confident, a small town in northern Minnesota, population 476, would be a welcoming place to raise a family. We were delighted to begin my first position in Rothsay, Minnesota, best known for the infamous Prairie Chicken statue. A recent graduate of Moorhead State University, I had accepted my first full-time job teaching first grade. From our good-natured neighbors to a close-knit family of teaching colleagues, our sixteen years in Rothsay were truly memorable.

More than anything, I wanted to live in the town I would be teaching in. However, when we went to buy our first home, there were not many houses to choose from in a town of less than 500. In fact, there were only two or three available. Even more, we were surprised as we signed the papers on our first house and discovered it came with a handyman and groundskeeper. The older gentleman, who resided in the backyard building, came with the property. Plus, as long as we owned the house, he would live there, rent-free.

His name was Eddie, and he was 85 years old. Knowing he did not pay us rent, Eddie felt obligated to mow the grass, rake leaves, and shovel the sidewalks. I was sixty years his junior; it was hard for me to let someone else do the jobs you thought were reserved for the man of the house. Still, I was not going to argue with this sweet old man. It was an amazing arrangement for the time we lived there. Eddie kept grinning as we filled the back yard with kids, a wooden swing set that Deb's dad built, and a sandbox. Even when we installed a fence in the backyard after Deb started a home daycare, Eddie adapted with each season. He always kept the lawn well-manicured and the snowy sidewalks cleared for daily daycare drop-offs.

One late frigid wintery night, we were stirred awake by a popping and crackling coming from our backyard. As we stood in our dining room, we had a direct view of the rear of the local hardware store. Deb and I were shocked to see flames shooting out of the store's electrical box. Within minutes the entire wall of this historic building was ablaze. We watched from the safety of our home as the city fire department worked frantically to keep the fire from spreading to other buildings. The temperatures were well below zero and dropping as the firemen worked throughout the night. By morning, the burned-out shell of the building was entombed in icicles. A river of ice had formed from the water running down the hill, flowing right into our garage, as well as flooding the path to the front door of Eddie's house.

I could hear him shouting; he was not able to open his door and was trapped inside. After chipping away with my ax, I was able to free him. It was such a bizarre chain of events that morning ending with me chiseling away at the 2-inch-thick sheet of ice, entrapping all four of our car tires. Hearing Eddie pounding and, shouting, I realized the poor old guy's door was sealed shut by layers of ice. That is an event that will always be stored in my memory bank.

A Small-Town Life

Miranda was only eight months old when we first arrived in Rothsay. With most new jobs, I wanted to impress, so I did more than just teach first grade. I was coaching speech, as well as directing the school musical, the all-school play, and the one-act play. With so many rehearsals to manage, there were several times Miranda would accompany me to play practice in her car seat. During practice, my group of enthusiastic young actors would keep Miranda engaged so I could direct the others. When we brought Miranda to the home volleyball and basketball games, some of the older girls would just whisk away our little girl and keep her entertained. It was the best part-time babysitting service one could ask for and a pleasant place to raise a daughter.

My early educational years in Rothsay were jam-packed with teaching, coaching, and directing. Even my summers were dedicated to studying. One summer, we traveled to Disney World in Florida, with our fellow friend and former teacher, Faith, and her three kids. The two educators could not pass through a state without making a pitstop at the capitol buildings or other historical landmarks. A teacher never stops learning.

Deb's days adequately provided a working parent's need as one of the home daycares in town. More importantly, Deb's business adventure supplied Miranda with a multitude of playmates.

Even so, Miranda's earliest and kindest memories were of Kindergarten and one the town's favored teachers, Jane Eklund. Her Kindergarten teacher had crafted a collection of numbered shoe boxes, each encompassing an exercise in cooperative play. Miranda cherished how each box held precious lessons fostering the traits of a unified family. For the most part, the academics of strategically identifying letters with corresponding sounds, as well as the significance of operations and number relationships still maintained importance. However, in Mrs. Eklund's Kindergarten, playing well together was paramount over math facts and letter formation. This simpler life of kindred bonding is one that Miranda will always treasure.

Each September brought the beginning of a new school year. However, in the fall of 1986, the year Miranda started Kindergarten, I lost someone very dear to me. My youngest sister Karen died unexpectedly from a pulmonary embolism. It was so sudden, so painful. There were times when I was so devasted, I did not want to get out of bed, let alone teach. My colleagues, my friends, rallied around and supported me. If I ever needed to take a moment because something reminded me of my sweet sister, one of them would step into my classroom, and take over the lesson until I could compose myself.

I will forever be grateful for the many ways that my Rothsay friends and colleagues helped me through that year.

Memories, pleasant or unpleasant, will fade in and out of your mind like the seasons of the year. For Miranda, her summers were filled with fond remembrances of the many friends she had solidified during the school year. It was not uncommon for Miranda, after shedding her PJs for shorts and a T-shirt, to be out the door and off on her bike. During those long days of summer, Miranda or her siblings would frequently shout goodbyes in the morning, and we would not see them again until dusk. The cozy town of Rothsay, about 200 households, spanned roughly 6 blocks long and 8 blocks wide. As Miranda's Mom and Dad, we personally knew the families our kids begged to spend their vacation days with. What we originally felt as an invasion of privacy, as parents, we had later come to appreciate and recognize as a blessing. The first time we got a call from a neighborly resident, the message went something like this, "We saw Miranda and her friends playing on the tracks. We wanted to make sure you were both okay with that. Or, did you want us to send her home?" We came to embrace the idea that so many towns-folk would take the time to watch over our children and keep us informed of their summer whereabouts.

For a teacher in Minnesota, June, July, and August were reserved for rejuvenation before school started after Labor Day. For a teacher, this was something to look forward to. Summer was also the time that Miranda's younger brother, Evan, and little sister Abby, both celebrated July birthdays. With birthdates only four days apart, their annual summer parties were often held on the same day. Miranda recalls a water slide in the backyard, separating one section of the yard for the boys and another section for the girls. Miranda would always beam when we gave her permission to invite one friend to partner with during the joint festivities. Summertime was also slated for swimming. One favorite spot was Big Cormorant

Lake where my parents had earned the title of Grandma and Grandpa Lake. When we traveled to southern Minnesota to see Grandma Maxine and Grandpa Golfcarting, Miranda loved the nearby community pool.

Leaves ablaze in vibrant shades of orange, yellow and red, usually brought the start of school and the time to shake apples from our backyard apple tree. Miranda reminded me that she and her siblings would spend hours climbing and then relaxing in the branches of our hearty fruit tree. One of Miranda's favorite jobs was to have someone lay down sheets around the tree, while she would climb as far as she could go and then frantically shake the limbs of the tree, watching the apples fall and bounce on the sheets then roll into the grass. What happened next was another treasured memory. The kids would gather all the apples and bring them to the kitchen. We had acquired an old-fashioned clamp-on apple peeler. The device could be mounted and tightened on the counter with a stainless-steel clamp. The kids took turns skinning after Deb or I would skewer the apple on the end of the peeling fork. Whoever first called dibs would start turning the wooden hand crank as the thin skins of the apples would fall to one side. Eating the ringlets of fresh apple skins was a tasty treat for the lucky peeler. Altogether, we would fill gallon containers with sliced apples for future pies, muffins, cobblers, crisps, or boiled down for sauces or jams. This shared time together as a family was priceless.

Routinely, this season was set aside to busily prepare for a new group of students, while my children were anxious to rejoin their old classmates. Miranda, the supreme student, journeyed through her elementary years with simplicity. Academically, Miranda tackled most subjects with incredible ease and according to countless teachers, "gets along well with others." In sixth grade, unfortunately, her winning streak would abruptly change. Miranda would be the first of my children to have her dad in his new role as the sixth-grade teacher.

As Miranda recalls, she had every reason to believe her sixth-grade year would be a walk in the park. Most of her friends and classmates had been to our home. Most knew and liked me personally, as Miranda would later corroborate, the year should have been a positive experience with her dad.

A few weeks into the school year, as expected, Miranda was pulling A's and B's, mostly A's. Even though her classmates had seen this all before, surprisingly, I heard some of them quietly commenting on Miranda's graded papers. Any assignments bearing the letter A received a snarky comment from her female classmates. With only 18 students making up her class, this repeated negative chatter could be difficult for any child. I tried a variety of discreet ways to return graded work to the students, but her classmates were relentless, accusing Miranda of getting special treatment and undeserved grades. As the resolute educator in our family, I had always been the one to assist with homework, projects, research; you name it, I was on it. This year, unpleasantly for Miranda, would not be a walk in the park. Trying to give her a foot to stand on with her friends, I basically refused to help Miranda during non-school hours. Deb had to take on this role, and this just made Miranda more frustrated. Miranda thought Mom's role was reserved for picking out cute outfits or teaching her how to bake. Dad's role was to aid in picking out the research topics or cooking up ways to prepare for an exam. I was supposed to make the sixth grade a superior year; I was failing miserably in Miranda's eyes.

Surviving the school year without her Dad's customary academic support was a challenge. A greater challenge lay ahead when Miranda moved into Junior High. According to our daughter, this became an unsettling time for her, as Miranda was negatively hurled into a world of injustice. Her catalyst was ushered in when a new student arrived in Rothsay. In a small town, when a new family moves in, everyone gossips about it. All of them optimistically anticipated a new addition might bring a blessing. In his case, Miranda would describe her new classmate as evil, pure evil. His wickedness began with sly, devious remarks whispered out of the reach of a teacher's ear. His dark utterances were carnal in nature, incessantly referencing parts of her body. His dispiriting words left Miranda distressed and uncomfortable in her own skin. As the days came and went with no teacher intervention, his lewd commentary referenced unsolicited sexual acts. Miranda was shamed into wearing larger sweatshirts and sweatpants in order to hide the outlines of her body. Each day he deliberately calculated the location and the minutes for his vulgar verbalizations. Sadly, no good-hearted neighbors were coming to her rescue this time. Miranda was adrift in our close-knit community. Our desolate daughter made her first complaint to the school office. Revealing the sordid details with a fragmented heart, Miranda was told by her new principal, she did not know this boy's story. For some reason, if Miranda was more aware of his sad account, it would explain away his actions or his obscene, crude comments.

Miranda finally shared all this information with her mother, a more likely confidant. There are reports of animals in the wild that intensely protect their young. Miranda witnessed a mama bear in action, unleash an internal rage that was uninhibited and unrestrained. When Deb arrived at the school, she found this boy, cornered him, and emphatically informed him, if he ever spoke to her daughter again, his days would be numbered; his world would become a nightmare. As she left the school, the boy was already jogging toward the school office. That evening, Miranda had one last sympathizer to recruit her dad.

The next morning, my principal called me to his office to tell me I needed to control my wife and her bully-like behavior. I took a very deep breath and forewarned my boss I was about to take off my teacher hat. With my dad hat firmly planted, I informed my principal I would not be reprimanding my wife because I applauded her browbeating. Someone at this school needed to do something about this boy. Furthermore, if I had known about his behavior earlier, I would have removed him from the classroom, then I would remove him from the school, and I would prefer if he was removed from this earth. My boss sputtered, "You don't understand; he's had a tough life." I held up my hand to stop him from speaking, "Do not talk to me about suffering a tough life. Not every lousy childhood gives you permission to speak to young women with such a distasteful mouth. Bad parenting does not need to define you!"

This showdown happened on a Friday morning and I percolated all day and all weekend. By Monday, it was all over. Like a debilitating high-grade fever, this wicked boy had arrived, and then he was gone. Over the weekend, his dreadful family drove off into the night and disappeared into the darkness.

Living in a town of less than 500, you knew there were bigger towns out there. I was getting restless, so I started looking for teaching jobs in other parts of the state. I simply wanted a change. Even though I was ready, I was not certain Deb, or the kids, were ready to move on. Surprisingly, Miranda shared, "I think you were ready for a change at the same time I was." We were both hoping for something more. Miranda added, "With only a few select friends in a small class, if you were on the outs with one classmate, everybody knew about it."

Those harrowing weeks of evil still bring tears to Miranda's eyes, resulting in a heart more guarded than ever. It probably did not help when Miranda accidentally picked up the house phone and discovered we might be moving. She overheard me, setting up an interview with the public-school system in southern Minnesota. Even though no one offered me a job on that call, Miranda understood, it was time to move on. Miranda finished her freshman year in a small town and prepared for her Sophomore year in a city ten times larger.

I hoped that Miranda had survived one of her first great challenges. With one unsolicited experience behind her,

Miranda did not have much say in this choosing, even after I decided to move our family across the state. One big choice, one of her own making, would come in her senior year.

High School Horror Story

We were moving and Miranda was going to be a sophomore in a new high school. At the school office, when registering for her classes, Miranda mentioned she wanted to play sports. Miranda had previously played volleyball and basketball. When she walked into the high school gym, a coach immediately came up to Miranda and tried to recruit her to play basketball. She hinted that she was not ready to commit to a winter sport, yet. Hoping to make her feel welcomed, the coach introduced Miranda to her son and his best friend. Miranda remembers thinking, she was the new kid in town, and sports could be her way in. At her first volleyball practice, Miranda met Jenny. When Miranda told us about the kids she met, about Jenny, I quizzed my new teacher buddies the next day. My informants said, Jenny was a party girl, and she was bad news. Great!

In her classes, Miranda met another girl, Sarah. They became fast friends. Within days, Miranda found two new friends, and she was living two separate lives. Sarah and Miranda were study buddies in school and sat by each other in class. Jenny and Miranda were teammates on the court. Sarah's friends were all cheerleaders and Jenny's friends were all volleyball players. Miranda was thinking, "I'm good. I was happy in both worlds."

Partway through the school year, Miranda started working at the Dairy Queen™. In our family, if you wanted spending money, you had to earn it. Most of the time at work, it was Miranda and three other high school kids. She found them all extremely funny and it did not take long for the four of them (Miranda, Carissa, Brandon, and Brian) to become besties and they loved to hang out together, in and out of the DQ™. Her mom and I could see, Miranda was having a good time with all these new friends. Then Miranda started dating a guy, but it did not appear to be maturing into a healthy relationship. I had my doubts.

There was one time when Miranda got sick, really sick. She could not go to school and certainly could not go to work. Her new work besties – Brian and Brandon —showed up at our house with a bowl of chicken noodle soup. After they left, I thought to myself, "there are boys who really do that kind of stuff." Her current boyfriend would never be that thoughtful. We believe it was after that realization, her thoughts about who she was dating, shifted. We knew Miranda deserved to be treated with respect. Who knew, one thoughtful bowl of chicken noodle soup would help her see more clearly. I started believing it might be time for Miranda to unguard her heart.

For Miranda, work became a great place to not only earn some quick cash but also build those solid, lasting relationships with some forever friends. One day, with no customers in the DQ™, the two guys and Miranda were goofing around. Brandon decided to spray her with the washer hose and then Brian shoved her in the freezer. When they finally let Miranda out, she pretended to be mad, really mad. Miranda gave them the full silent treatment. For several minutes, which probably felt like hours to these boys, Miranda did not say one word. Miranda was pretty sure they thought they had crossed a line and she was beyond upset. The next thing she saw was both guys outside the front of the store pulling several blooms from the flower boxes. They came back inside and hurriedly put the stems in a makeshift Blizzard cup vase. Then, they took a plastic sundae container and filled it with the chocolate toppings the Dairy Queen™ used for Blizzards. Together, they sheepishly presented Miranda with "flowers and chocolates." This was another unguarded moment; good boys can care about young women and that can be nice to hear about. Miranda knew she had to break it off with my current boyfriend.

Word soon spread that Miranda was single. One day at the DQ™, Brandon motioned her over and said, "There's somebody that likes you and he wants to go on a date with you." Not sure where this was going, Miranda surveyed his face and responded with a tiny timid "okay." Brandon continued, "There's one problem. I like you too." Miranda realized what was happening, Brandon was asking her out for Brian, not for himself. With little fanfare, Miranda agreed, and Brian and Miranda went on a date. They tried the dating thing for about two weeks. It only took a few dates to realize, Brian and Miranda would just be forever friends, and they still are. Brian is happily married and has four beautiful children.

Miranda started spending more time with Brandon away from the DQ™. They found they could talk for hours and hours and hours. Miranda came to realize her sentiments for Brandon were starting to shift after he told her, "there's one problem." They started as classmates, became work buddies and but she could sense her feelings for him were changing. It was the beginning of their Senior year in high school and together they had so much to look forward to.

Brandon was playing football. During the games, we all got to know his family. Around the time the football season was coming to an end, Brandon told Miranda his parents were planning their annual vacation to Hawaii. His parents informed him, as a senior and in honor of his 18th birthday, they would take him to Hawaii, and he could bring whoever he wanted to. Brandon told them he picked Miranda. Not sure how we would receive the news, Miranda finally got up the courage to ask. She explained that she would be traveling with Brandon's parents as well as Brandon's aunt and uncle. Their travel group would be two married couples and two high school seniors. Brandon turned eighteen in October, and Miranda would turn eighteen in December before they all left on the trip. We were okay with arrangements with one stipulation, Miranda had to pay for the trip herself. When she looked at what she had in savings and what she would earn before they all left, Miranda knew she had enough money to pay her share.

Always the educator, always the rule follower; I informed Deb and Miranda, "You need to notify the school you'll be missing three days of classes before winter break." In hindsight, perhaps they should have ignored me and asked for grace later. Deb wrote the note, and Miranda brought it to school. By the end of the day, Deb got a call to come to the High School office. The administration wanted to talk. The principal and dean of students sat Deb and Miranda down and informed them that they had decided, Miranda could not go on this trip because she would miss too many days. Even though her parents had granted their permission to go, the school was saying they would count all three days as unexcused. Deb asked what would be considered excused by school policy. One of the administrators informed us that preapproved family vacations could be excused. However, they reminded us they always had the final say on approving any days.

Next, one of the administrators leaned in and questioned Deb. "How could a parent allow their daughter to go on an unsupervised trip with her boyfriend? Only an immoral parent would allow this." This same administrator went on to say if we permitted Miranda to go, they would have no choice but to suspend her. She would not be allowed to make up the work and, therefore, would fail each the classes Miranda was enrolled in. Miranda and Deb tried to rationalize in their heads what they were saying. Her schedule for the remainder of the year was one English class, one math elective, an art elective, and three study halls. Miranda had excellent grades. She was one of the students in line for school valedictorian. The handbook said, "Students who have excused absences will be required to make up missing hours in before/after school study program. Failure to complete the hours may result in loss of privileges and/or suspension." Miranda hadn't even left yet, and these administrators were saying if she went, they would suspend her, or worse, flunk her.

Deb and I knew that seniors, as per the handbook, were allowed two days for college visits. After Deb had time to process, she called some colleges in Hawaii and scheduled two tours. Deb was thinking, if we approved that, perhaps the school would grant at least one day as an excused absence. Still frustrated the next morning, Deb shared what had transpired at the school and told some of her colleagues at work. Deb did not know that one of the people she talked to at work was close to one of the administrators and her colleague contacted the school and forewarned the administrator about her idea to propose the college visits.

The next day, the administration requested another meeting with both Deb and Miranda. The same two administrators proceeded to tell Deb it was ridiculous to visit any colleges in Hawaii, any visit to a college would be unexcused. They were prepared for this suggestion and dismissed it. Deb left the meeting in tears; she was so frustrated and angry. Miranda was trying desperately to process all that had been said. There was no way the school could really do this. They could not. They should not, because they were wrong. We gave our daughter permission. They were traveling with four adults. Miranda did nothing wrong and this entire situation was getting ridiculous.

Deb and I asked her what she wanted to do. Miranda told us, she had met with the school guidance counselor and he went over each of her credits earned, and according to the High School Handbook, she had met all the requirements to graduate, except for a half credit of English. All the other classes Miranda was enrolled in were not required to graduate. Miranda had already fulfilled her electives. The guidance counselor had mentioned another option that was available to her. Miranda might be able to earn the English credit through a local university as a dual enrollment student. It was not that common in 1999, but it could be done.

Miranda said with determination, "I feel more than anything, we have done nothing wrong. You are not terrible parents. You are not immoral. I have worked hard to earn and maintain a 4.0 and if it was still okay with you, I want to go on the trip. I will still visit the colleges that mom made arrangements for. We can sort everything out when I return." Deb and I agreed; we supported Miranda's decision.

While on her trip the school informed Deb, they had prepared a couple of options:

Option 1: Miranda could simply withdraw from school.

We explained Miranda could not simply do that. She had already accepted college scholarships. If she withdrew or if the high school failed her, the college would decline Miranda her scholarships. We tried to explain they were putting Miranda's future in jeopardy with the University of Duluth, where she had already been accepted. Singlehandedly, they were destroying any chance at any future academic scholarships. With that being said, they proposed another possibility.

Option 2: Miranda could stay on as a part-time student but enroll in the alternative school's evening program to fulfill her required credit of English.

I decided to conduct an inquiry of my own and called a local lawyer who had represented some other students who had attended the same high school.

Interestingly, when Miranda returned from the trip, we were notified by the school to attend a third meeting. This time, a new person had joined the group; she was a local attorney. Her purpose during this session was to let all parties know that she had heard of the situation. She wanted to inform the high school administration that because Miranda was eighteen at the time of the trip, she was considered her own family. Therefore, Miranda did not need her parents or the school's permission to go on the trip. Because Miranda was an adult, any proposed absences should be excused, and in the best interest of all, our family and the school just needed to sort out the details for the half-credit of English to graduate.

It was rumored, the high school added a couple of new statements to their handbook the summer after Miranda's senior year.

Those students who are eighteen years of age and older will be expected to abide by the same rules and regulations that apply to the remainder of the student body. Student absences for eighteen-year-olds will still require parent /guardian verification. The only exception to this is for students who are legally independent and no longer claimed as dependents by the parent/guardian.

During her trip to Hawaii, Miranda had plenty of time to think about what to do when she returned. Miranda knew that she was not going to spend the rest of her senior year assigned to an in-school suspension, to show up every day, sit in solitary, away from her classmates. That made no sense to her or us. She was not excited about the alternative school. In her mind, it was the place where they sent all the badly behaved kids. The kids who could not cut it in regular school. Miranda kept comparing it to the Island of Misfit Toys from the old cartoon, Rudolph the Red Nose Reindeer. Miranda had landed on not returning to school and taking the dual enrollment option until I went to check out one of the classes at the alternative school.

After that visit, I suggested, "Go, see for yourself. Don't count it out, not just yet." I was the Community Education Director for the school district, and I knew the instructor personally. She oversaw the adult education classes for the school district, and I had talked with her at length while Miranda was on her trip. This teacher had made such an impression on me, I really hoped Miranda would go and meet her. Miranda said she trusted me more than the school administrators and the lawyers, so she went.

The alternative school met in the late afternoons and evenings. That would take some getting used to if Miranda decided to go there. Miranda learned that the classes were taught by a husband and wife team and they had been doing it for years. If she made the choice to take the English credit from her, Miranda would be the only one taking English, everyone else was enrolled in History. Miranda slipped into a desk in the back of the class and listened. The teacher was asking questions, quizzing, all the other students in the room and they were bouncing answers off each other. If the teachers wanted more detailed answers, another student would jump up and add on until the teacher was satisfied, they'd covered all the material. Miranda sat there realizing that she knew very few of the answers. Miranda had a 4.0 G.P.A. and she felt lost.

All of the sudden, Miranda made her next big choice. As she did, a wave of peace came over her. Miranda wanted to be in this class. She wanted to learn the way these students were learning. Miranda wanted more than anything to gain a better understanding of these people labeled misfits.

Miranda grasped that each one of her new classmates was special and unique in their own way. They were acquiring knowledge in a non-traditional format, and they were thriving. Miranda learned, not every child needs a traditional school setting. Her new study buddies shared how they felt pushed aside and tossed out of the same school system that cast Miranda aside. Nevertheless, here they all were flourishing. Every night this community made her feel welcomed by their friendly smiles. Her unguarded heart recognized these feelings again. Miranda was surrounded by well-intended neighborly faces. This group of mislabeled misfits had something she wanted too, personal pride. They emulated confidence; they were internally proud of themselves.

Because Miranda was attending class at night, she had her days free. The bank president where Deb worked, heard what had happened. His daughter had graduated the year before and he remembered Miranda. He offered Miranda a full-time job at the bank. So, she began her final semester as a High School Senior, attending night class and working full time as a bank teller. Everything had fallen into place until we got another call from the school telling us they had decided something else. Even though Miranda had earned my 4.0 before starting night school, she was no longer eligible for Valedictorian. Miranda would be able to walk at graduation, but she would not be receiving her honor cords.

The day of Miranda's graduation was an emotional one, to say the least. Even as a member of the school staff, Deb and I did not receive the usual invite for front row seating like the other parents of honor students about to walk across the stage. We sat in the back of the gym. As Miranda received her diploma, my eyes filled with tears. I took a deep breath and finally exhaled; the whole ordeal was finally over.

In retrospect, it was hard to find joy during the last half of her senior year. We do feel blessed in a few ways because Miranda did meet Brandon. There are some very dear friends we came to know and continue to cherish; like, Ken, Bev, Eldean, Nita, Deb, and Brad. They are simply good, God-loving people.

One summer, at a local community event, a colleague entered into a heated discussion with Deb and me and called "Bullshit." He accused us of trying to circumvent the school system. In the same vein, a coworker at Deb's bank had righteously quizzed her. "Who did your daughter think she was? Why did you two think you didn't have to follow the same rules as anybody else?" This prompted me to ask Miranda if we had to do it all over again, would you choose the same path and make the same choices?

I was reflecting with Miranda because I was not as confident as I had been when we were in the fray. I thought, "Did we really try to beat the system? Is this how people really saw us? We were so busy being right, is it possible, we were wrong?"

Even though, we as a family had made the final choice, I was no longer certain it was the right choice.

Miranda smiled and said, "Yes I would do it all over again. I would walk the same painful path. I would make the same choices."

Perhaps, my frustrated colleague was right. The whole jumbled mess was "Bullshit." No one had the right to call my wife immoral and imply that she was a terrible parent.

Maybe Deb's coworker was also right. It is not fair if you do not follow the rules. I am quite sure the school did not follow its own rules. Miranda had worked hard for her 4.0 G.P.A. She had already earned those honor cords for the work she had completed before she went to Hawaii. The school created its own new set of rules. They callously took that recognition away from Miranda.

I always knew schools were supposed to be places to learn. In the end, Miranda was humbled to learn that not all students acquire skills in the same way. For some, you need to take a different approach, a different path. You meet them where they are at. You strive to understand their story. You guide them, together and alone; allowing them to flourish with confidence. What we did not know at the time was that Miranda and her future husband, Brandon, would have to walk a similar path of uncertainty and critical choices. However, in this future journey, they would walk alongside each other, but this time, their troublesome trek would be focused on their eldest son.

6

HUNTING FOR PURPOSE

The best way to describe pregnancy number two was to use the word "blessed," according to Deb. She remembers being healthy and active right up until the time she went into labor. Our second child was due at the end of July. With the start of summer, I was off from teaching school and Deb was playing on a local softball team. I was coaching or keeping the books; not sure what you'd call it, mostly I was being a supportive spouse. The fact that Deb played softball just days before baby number two's arrival, should explain our son's eternal love for the game of baseball. He was probably cheering his mom on from the womb.

Evan Jay Sieling was born on July 28, 1983. Two extraordinary things occurred on the day of his birth. First, a tornado warning went off during our stay at the hospital and I had to retreat to a basement for shelter. When I could return to her floor, I learned Deb and our new baby had to wait in the hallway until the warning was over. Second, our extraordinary new baby was a BOY! We had a son. In fact, we had a girl and a boy. Our hearts were full.

First Son

Evan's earliest memories of being a member of the Sieling clan mostly stem from our second home in Rothsay. What Deb and I loved about this second house was its location in relation to the city park. This house also had an unfinished basement I could convert into living and working space for her booming daycare. A better heating and cooling system, amazing neighbors, and an apple tree in the backyard rounded out the positives of home number two. We did not inherit a handyman, a lawn keeper, or a snow removal guy, but this newer house offered plenty of space.

What we left behind was an old floorboard radiator heating system fueled by a huge wood-burning boiler. What we would not miss with the new house, was the immense amount of time we spent during the fall, chopping, splitting, and stacking logs in preparation for a Minnesota long cold winter. One of my most memorable moments with Evan happened on one of those frigid winter nights. In fact, the temperature was well below zero, and I was afraid the vent stack on our roof would ice over. I had just heard a precautionary story on the evening news about plumbing air vents, those meant to remove gas odors. The news story said vents could ice over in those frigid temperatures. One frozen vent had caused carbon monoxide fumes making the family extremely ill.

Not wanting a similar fate for my family; I put on my warmest clothes and boots and I carried the extension ladder near the side of the house that was closest to the bathroom vent. With a hammer hanging from my belt, I climbed the ladder up to the first roofline. Then, I hoisted up the ladder, carefully placed it in a pile of snow on the slippery roof, and climbed to the next level where I banged away at the vent until all the ice broke off. The descent was slippery and treacherous as I maneuvered the ladder on the snow-packed roofs before I finally reached the ground. It was late in the evening when

I finally got back inside the house. Exhausted, I did a sweep of the bedrooms to see if Miranda and Evan were asleep. I could see the outline of Miranda in her bed, but only an empty space where Evan should have been. I could feel the house had cooled down a bit during my outdoor quest. Before turning in, I would need to put another big log in the boiler to keep the house warm and cozy, preventing the pipes from freezing and find Evan.

As I reached the basement and moved into the room where the boiler was, there stood Evan in his Winnie the Pooh, blue fleece pajamas, and red rubber boots. He was trying with all his mini-might to push a log into the boiler. The door was wide open. I could see the inside of the boiler was aglow, and Evan was pushing and grunting as he tried to shove an enormous log into the firebox. I am quite sure I screamed his name because Evan turned around so quickly. I rushed to his side and pulled him back towards me. Evan must have seen a frightened and worried look on my face when he offered up, "I was trying to help keep the house warm." Evan was just two and a half and could have easily slipped inside the boiler door while trying to maneuver that log. I do not even want to think about what could have happened that night. I just made Evan promise to never to put logs into the boiler unless I was there to help or supervise.

When we finally retired the wooden boiler in our first house for an electric one; that was a good day. We no longer had to spend autumn weekends splitting and stacking wood or worry about helper Evan stoking the fire. When we moved across town to the "white house" as the kids called it, the first thing I noted with a satisfying smile, the heating system was already electric.

Miranda and Evan enjoyed the proximity to the city park as well, only a few hundred feet away from our front door. If Evan was not in the back-yard reenacting action scenes from his favorite Saturday morning cartoons, he would be at the city park, hanging out with his guy friends or riding his bike all over town. Even in a small town, being a "townie" had its benefits. Having mom operate a daycare in her home had even more benefits. Evan recalls he always had an ample supply of friends, thanks to Deb's Daycare. Evan's childhood buddies would stay close and remain good friends into his middle school and early high school years. He always wanted to spend time with his pal, Pat. At an incredibly young age, Pat and Evan vowed they would be friends forever and agreed they would be Best Man at each other's weddings. A sacred promise they did keep years later.

All Boy

Just like Miranda, Evan had Mrs. Eklund in Kindergarten. While Miranda cherished her academic and companionship memories, Evan happily remembers a time his class was preparing for a Hawaiian Luau and the girls had gone down to the bathroom to change into their age-appropriate summer tops and grass skirts. After changing into a floral shirt, and adorning a plastic floral lei, Evan waited in the hallway near the opened classroom door. Upon seeing the bevy of beauties coming back down the hallway, Evan announced to the guys, "Get ready, boys, here they come!" Evan appreciated the ladies in his life.

Another one of Evan's infamous lines came from the kids' cartoon, *He-Man and the Masters of the Universe*. In the same fashion as the cartoon, magical secret powers could be revealed to Evan when he would lift a cardboard sword, bat, or stick above his head and shout, "By the Power of Grayskull." Since this was one of the most popular kid's cartoons of the late 1980s, Evan viewed it faithfully. One summer Deb and I came across an artisan at the Phelps Mill craft fair who had crafted a wooden sword and a shield. I could not resist. I convinced Deb we needed to get it for Evan. He was so excited about our purchase, and it was entertaining to watch him yield his new treasures in the backyard. Evan slept with the sword and wanted to take his "weapons" every place we went.

In the winter of 1992, the Mall of America opened in Minneapolis, Evan insisted he would take his "weapons" with him on our family outing. Deb and I convinced him to keep the shield in the car, but we let Evan carry the sword if he agreed to tuck it close to his leg between the fabric loops of his pants and his belt. Evan had done such a good job of keeping his weapon at his side during lunch at the third level courtyard. Both Deb and I had forgotten to remind Evan to keep it at his side as we saw him move closer to the glass railing to look at mobs of people in one of the shopping areas below.

I did not notice his sword in his hand as he tried to pull himself up to the railing to get a better look. The sword suddenly slipped from his hand and plummeted out of sight, some 40 feet below. I reached the railing wide-eyed in time to see the sword land inches away from a baby in a stroller and bounce off the floor with a loud wood on tile "smack." I ran down a set of stairs, taking two at a time. As I reached the young mother, she was looking up at Deb, who was looking down yelling, "We are so sorry!" I picked up the sword (which miraculously had not splintered on impact) and I apologized profusely, repeatedly asked if she and her baby were okay. She was a bit confused but assured me, both were unharmed. Evan and I marched back to where we had the car parked with me half counseling, half scolding him all the way. Evan shared as we reached the car, he thought it was best if his "weapon' stayed with his shield. I agreed. We would have to get used to the idea that this kid always had something in his hand he was pushing, poking, prodding, hitting, or batting with.

For example, Evan equally reminisced about the pleasures of having an apple tree in the back yard. Both Miranda and Evan had similar sweet memories of peeling apples so Mom could bake every apple-related desert from the famous, Rothsay Cookbook. On the other hand, what Evan enthusiastically remembers was something more appealing to him. After Deb told him no more apples, she had canned and frozen enough, Evan would pick the apples off the ground and use them for batting practice. Leave it to Evan, all boy, as he would smash the ripe fruit into thousands of pieces after connecting with the bat. Evan would point towards the back yard or alley, throw the apple in the air, and swing away.

As Evan moved through his later elementary years, he loved playing all kinds of sports with the kids in his class before the start of the school day. He usually found himself being one of the last people to leave the playground and head into class. For Evan, playing kickball, tag, kill the carrier, or touch football, was the best part of the school day. He was that kind of son most dads envision when they first hear they are going to have a baby boy. As a dad, you are excited about someone to wrestle with, to be rough-and-tumble with. However, sometimes Evan took rough-and-tumble to a new extreme. I am happy to report I had nothing to do with his reckless run of injuries.

In fourth grade, sport-loving Evan got sacked before school started. He clearly recalls the tackle hurt on impact but not enough to stop playing. That afternoon when he got home, Deb noticed he was favoring his left side, looking rather stiff, and his left arm was hanging at his side. When Deb tried to touch his shoulder, she could see he winced in pain. With a quick trip to the local doctor, he was able to push his dislocated shoulder back into place. Evan would have to wear a sling for the next few weeks.

This incident was probably Evan's first memorable encounter with "Big Red," the name Deb earned when her Momma Bear came out. Evan remembers feeling nervous going back to school the next day after hearing "Big Red" scold his teacher over the phone for letting Evan sit in class all day with a dislocated shoulder. "Big Red" could not believe his teacher had not noticed Evan was in pain most of the day.

The summer between his fourth-grade and fifth-grade year, Evan decided to start skateboarding. He was doing fine until he tried to catch himself with his outstretched hand as he fell off the moving skateboard, dislodging his thumb. After coming back from the same doctor's office, Evan continued to practice skating with a shiny, aluminum splint protecting his sprained thumb. I guess the tough just keep going.

One of our favorite local hangouts, when summer arrived, was Pebble Beach in Fergus Falls. A stretch of sandy beach and playground provided plenty of entertainment for our kids. There was a set of monkey bars at the beach Evan thought he could master while hanging upside down. After he fell from the bars to the hard-packed earth below, Evan tried to dust himself with both hands. As I moved toward Evan, he was holding up his arm with a strange look on his face. I could clearly see my son was not okay. I think the best way to describe what I saw was a dent or a dip beyond his wrist where a straight bone should be. This was now our third trip to the doctor's office or an emergency room in a few months.

As a result, we should not have been surprised as Evan was enthusiastically retelling stories of his dislocated shoulder, sprained thumb, and now broken arm, to the doctor and nurses. One nurse turned toward me, and I saw the look. The nurse quietly asked me to step outside the room and informed me they were concerned Evan's so-called accidents were so close together and appeared to be a bit suspicious. It took me a few seconds to connect the dots and understand what I was being accused of as I assured the nurse and doctor that these were all boy related accidents and, in no shape or form, were any of these questionable incidents intentional physical abuse. These two health care workers did not know me; they had no idea how they had stirred up something deep inside me. Deep-seated memories, long before my children were born, emotions kept at bay for years. I was a good father. I would never deliberately hurt my son. Their nonchalant allegations were devastating to hear. They did not know me. They did not know what we had experienced growing up. We never reported suspicious incidents to anyone. I had long buried episodes of burns, welts, and bruises. Up until this day, those painful memories had stayed hidden and locked away. Luckily, I did not have to explain any further. Evan's elaborate storytelling convinced the Emergency Room staff his incidents had been exactly what they were: "a boy, being a boy" accidents.

Middle School Move

After his season of injuries, Evan's elementary years transitioned into middle school. Evan found himself in the same predicament Miranda had to endure; his dad was going to be his sixth-grade teacher as well. Evan and Miranda both agreed, they received a similar talk at home right before their sixth-grade year started. The primary reason for the conversation, I did not want Evan to experience the same undeserved treatment his sister received at the hands of his peers. To prevent that, at home. I would still be Dad; at school, I was Mr. Sieling or Mr. S.

They were blessed; both Miranda and Evan were quality scholars, and schoolwork came easy to them. After the first quarter of school, I could readily see Evan would do fine academically. However, among his peers, father and son had to be careful, so it did not come across as though I was showing Evan favoritism. My previous encounters with Miranda's peers reverberated inside my psyche. If I did demonstrate even the smallest of bias, life with his classmates would be more challenging. The distinct difference, Evan was a guy; his peers were not as cruel with their comments and less likely to offer up "Daddy's Favorite" or "Daddy's Girl." If the cynicism occurred, Evan could shrug it off more quickly than his older sister. His memories of sixth-grade were slightly a bit more positive. He took full advantage of getting to go to school early or stay late to hang out longer on the playground because I was a teacher. For Evan, he considered his constant hall pass to be a true perk.

In seventh-grade, we all made the move to Glencoe. Evan was not excited about this change, not at all. The anticipated separation from his childhood friends, his amigos, would be more painful than any broken arm. Like the slim pickings from our first home, there were fewer real estate choices. Moving to a bigger town did not improve our housing situation. Still, right before the school year started, we did find an unappealing but practical mouse-infested farmhouse to rent. Each morning, the kids would ride with me to their schools, and then I would go off to my job, teaching fourth grade. One morning, I had a good viewpoint of Evan in my rear-view mirror. It was pretty somber by the time I dropped Evan off that morning.

It was not just the look; the tears rolling down his face gave me enough incentive to call the Junior High principal. In our short phone call, I told the principal I was worried about Evan, the transition to a new town, his lack of good friends, and his general feeling of melancholy. On our drive home, Evan reported the principal had called him into his office. Evan was surprised to see another student was already there. After some small talk, the principal assured Evan things would eventually get better. The principal offered Evan some encouragement and assured him new friends were right around the corner, as he introduced Evan to a fellow classmate. Evan assumed the other kid would have been labeled the "nice guy" or "popular" back then, but after they both walked out the door, Evan said the "nice guy" didn't speak to him again until Evan starting playing fall football.

Even though Evan thought he was not big enough to play fullback, he volunteered to play the position because he knew he was small enough and fast enough to run between other players during the scrimmages. In one game he had made a long run for a touchdown and few more noticeable plays in future games. In a way, sports more or less became his saving grace. Some of the guys and gals started talking to Evan in the hallways and in his classrooms. Eventually, some relationships did get better, but the friendships were not deep-rooted like Rothsay. Evan learned, in a larger town, in a larger school, he could rotate friends. So, his collection of buddies, peers, classmates, and friends moved in and out through different times of the year. Evan had his various rotations with his end of summer pals, his friends at the Burger King, the winter snoball court, and his wrestling squad. Spring would usher in new baseball teammates and, in the fall, another season of hunting buddies.

The Joy of Hunting

One of Evan's earliest recollections of the art of hunting happened when he was working his job at Burger King. Two of his classmates came into the fast-food place all dressed in camouflage. After a general inquiry of what they were doing, what area, how often; they finally invited Evan to go along. Let us just say, he fell in love with this outdoor pastime. Next to baseball, hunting has been a passion of his. Evan would have to figure out how to gather up the supplies. I did not own a single gun and had no desire to have one in the house. Perhaps, I was still gun shy after Larry's accident.

Evan was determined to hunt with his friends, but he had no hunting gear, no camouflage, and no gun. Luckily for Evan, I had six brothers who had all of that. One of them had an old twelve gauge, and he offered it to Evan. Thanks, brother. Whenever Evan was not working, participating in a fall, winter, or spring sport, he was hunting or thinking about ways to make money to buy more hunting equipment.

After we moved to Chandler, Arizona, Evan got a job with BIG 5 Sporting Goods. He was so happy to learn he would even receive a BIG 5 discount. With his first paycheck, Evan began buying hunting gear to better serve his obsessive passion for killing birds. Near the time of his senior high school graduation, he was tinkering with the idea of community college but never nailed down which school he was looking at. As his parents, we had an idea his hunting trip to Minnesota in the fall may have influenced Evan to consider an out of state choice. We were not surprised to learn Evan had already conducted a campus visit to Aakers Business College in Fargo, North Dakota. We knew the call of the Midwest was all around us when we came home one night and heard a duck call in our back yard. In our pool, we found Evan, sitting in an inflatable raft, surrounded by a flock of floating goose decoys of different sizes. He was so busy trying out his new goose call he didn't notice us until we shouted his name. After he thoroughly explained the purpose of each decoy in the pool, Deb and I walked back into the house. There was no way our son was going to stay in Arizona. The geese of North Dakota were calling his name and he was ready to leave the nest.

Not long after he started classes at Aakers, Evan got a text from his best pal, Pat; a good buddy of his. Pat had found an ad in the newspaper for a waterfowl hunting guide in the Dakotas. Back then, potential bosses listed phone numbers to call if you wanted to inquire about the job or schedule an interview. So, Evan called the number. Taking advice from one of his business teachers, Evan put together a formal résumé, dressed up in a button-down shirt, a tie, a nice pair of tan khakis, and some dress shoes for his interview at a hunting guide.

It took four hours to drive to the lodge, and Evan got lost a few times trying to locate the right roads. When he pulled up to the building, he saw someone coming down the stairs, probably there to greet him. The guy was dressed in jeans, a flannel shirt, and work boots. Before Evan left the car, he slipped off his tie, dropped it in the front seat, and reached over and grabbed a cloth bag holding his goose calls.

Evan soon learned the guy walking towards him was the son of the owner. As he reached out his hand, he announced, "You must be Evan." The son could see Evan was carrying a manilla folder in his other hand. The guy guessed "Is that your résumé? Well, you probably will not need that, my dad already read it. You impressed the shit out of my dad on the phone. I think I've only done that two times in my life, so you are off to a good start. Come on in!"

Evan sat down at the table ready to further impress the owner. He started the conversation by telling Evan to relax, "You already have the job." The owner declared, "You walk in with a résumé. This means you are treating this interview like a business. That is exactly what we are, a family business. I don't really need to ask more questions. I just want to get to know my new employee." After leaving the interview and knowing that he would be starting a job as a hunting guide, Evan felt he had just been drafted by the Minnesota Twins baseball team. He could not believe someone was going to pay him to hunt at nineteen years old.

His first year was a blissful blur. Every guide was provided with a Suburban, a trailer full of decoys, waders, and several other needed essentials. As well as two hunting dogs; a lab, and a setter. As the guide, Evan would start his day with one of the assigned groups staying at the lodge. The lodge had a big following of numerous hunters from all around the country, even as far south as the Carolinas. The groups would typically rotate in three-day intervals, as one group left another would come in. Now and then, some groups even flew into the local airport on their own private planes. Evan saw firsthand, up close, and personal, to what extreme other people would go who had a similar passion for killing birds.

Evan's routine went something like this: After eating a big breakfast, Evan would take the groups on their goose hunts in the morning. Then after a light lunch, it was pheasant and upland hunting in the afternoon. Next, Evan would take the goose and duck hunters back out and set them up in a pothole, while he and the other guides would drive around the countryside looking for the best places to hunt the next morning.

In the evening he would take each of the groups back to the lodge and bring the kill of the day down to the "bird boys" to be cleaned.

Evan was wide-eyed in years one and two. He often worked for thirty days with hunters coming and going without having any breaks. In year two, Evan became aware of a trend happening with the big spenders; those who came with big tips and private planes. After a day of hunting, the "bird boys" would throw some of the birds in tubs. Evan noticed a few times that they would not clean all the birds, simply tossing them in the tubs. By law, because most fowl are federal birds, if you shoot it, you must keep it. You receive limits when you purchase your hunting license. Every hunter is aware, you are only allowed so many birds in your possession identified by the limit provided on the license.

Depending on how many were in the hunting party, what the daily limit allowed, each person with a license would have their number of allotted birds thrown in their group buckets for cleaning. Each of these birds would then get cleaned by the "Bird Boys." The "Bird Boys" would leave a wing to identify the type of bird. After cleaning, the birds would be bagged, then placed in the lodge freezer for the hunters to take home when they left.

In his third year, the family that ran the lodge, still happy with Evan's work ethic, asked him if he wanted to manage the south lodge. In the first few weeks of his new role, Evan was bringing back two clients from the fields when he saw ten or so government cars parked all around the lodge. Evan could make out one of his former clients coming down the stairs, now wearing a Federal Game and Fish uniform. The light bulb went off. Evan connected the dots; his former client was an undercover agent. Evan recalls, when hunting with this client, he asked a boatload of pointed questions about the lodge, how things were run, even asked if he could see where the "Bird Boys" cleaned the kill of the day. Evan later learned the Federal

Game and Fish guys had a warrant and were talking to all the people at the lodge. While the group was waiting to get interviewed, the guides started speculating, "Our clients shot too many birds." His fellow guides continued, "Our clients are businessmen. Face it guys, they just wanted to pay money, come in, kill some birds, and go home. Our customers never intended to take their birds back home with them. Plus, our boss was not going to force paying clients — our biggest tippers — to take their birds home."

Every guide had their chance to tell their story. The undercover agent told Evan; he had not done anything illegal during the hunts when he was with Evan. However, the agent was concerned Evan had knowingly participated in "pitching or tossing the birds." During his interrogation, Evan admitted he had seen it happen. Evan was later charged with "Guilt by Association for Unlawful Transportation of Migratory Waterfowl." Evan was charged with a misdemeanor, was assigned a probation officer, and had to pay a twelve hundred dollar fine.

Before his sentencing, Evan's lawyer told him he would probably lose his hunting license, his guns, and not be allowed to hunt again for two years. On the day of his sentencing, Evan entered the courtroom in Minot, to find the arresting Game and Fish officer waiting in the room. Evan was told by the judge he was going to Skype in from the state capitol in Bismarck. The Game and Fish officer greeted Evan, asked how Evan was doing, and then asked if he could speak on Evan's behalf to the judge. Evan thought this was a strange request, but he was eager to hear what the officer had to say. After swearing-in, the officer leaned into the camera and spoke, "Could we start Evan's probation in December? This guy will not be able to hunt for the next two years. We will be taking away something from a guy who really loves to do this. I was hoping we could let Evan have this fall to hunt again with his friends. We can start his probation in December or January." With little hesitation, the judge agreed.

Evan only served probation for eleven months of the full eighteen months he was sentenced. Evan could keep his guns if he agreed to lock them up during his probation. As his parents, we understood what Evan was accused of, what he had admitted to; according to the agent, the act was unlawful. As dedicated foster parents, we have tried to make sense of the charges brought against our son. We never fully understood why judges or courts would hear a case about pitching or tossing birds. It was hard to comprehend why a person who was aware of the practice had to be sentenced and fined. We have repeatedly sat in the courts and heard horrible stories of how adults abandon or toss aside their own children. It is obvious the biological parents have made poor choices, otherwise, the children would not be removed. Yet, again and again, they are allowed to schedule visits with their kids each week. Rarely do they have to pay a fine. They hardly ever serve probation. Our experience of fostering over thirty-five children finds most of the biological parents continue to abuse alcohol or drugs, miss scheduled visits, and will eventually be severed from their children. With that planted firmly in our minds, we simply cannot wrap our heads around the idea that migratory birds have more rights than Arizona's children.

Getting Goosed

One of the rewards of hunting, according to Evan, was the sound or pitch of a good goose call. Evan knows, speaking goose takes practice, takes time, and takes discipline. The dividends of his labors, as he honed his goose-calling prowess, could make the difference between an endless string of birdless days or satisfied clients in the goose fields. To use this instrument —this flute — to control a flock of geese was so personally gratifying for Evan. To turn a flock of geese in a midair formation, to bring them in, held an exceptional place in his goose calling heart. Reading the movement of these beautiful birds in flight was part of Evan's field forte. To his joy, Evan's clients amply acknowledged their guide's competence with big-hearted tips, as well as profound praises.

While at Aakers Business School, Evan crossed paths with another student when he noticed rival decals on his truck window. The labels caught his eye because some were the best-known calls on the market. After some back and forth banter, they learned each would be competing in the same local call competition. This new fellow caller placed third and Evan placed fourth. They both decided about the same time, what if they teamed up and entered a few two-man competitions. In the same area, they met a thirteen-year-old kid who was nicknamed "Little Man." He was a good caller and was doing quite well in the junior circuit.

One summer, between seasons at the lodge, Evan was working as a Pro-staffer, promoting decoys and equipment as well as participating in some of the local call competitions. It was a small circuit in the Dakotas. As they moved from show to show, this new trio started making a name for themselves. In fact, they were a triple threat, as they racked up several trophies.

The new triad traveled to different competitions together. "Little Man" was winning the junior contests; his fellow caller was winning first or second. In addition, Evan was usually taking second or third in the senior single men match ups. In the two men competitions, their trio would usually take top honors with varying combinations between Evan, his fellow caller, and "Little Man." They were usually walking away with first, second, or third in most of the goose call battles.

Throughout their winning summer, this trio was using a goose call being manufactured out of someone's garage. With the feedback the trio received from the judges, Evan and his fellow caller started making suggestions to their garage-based manufacturer. The producers heard what the guys said but never moved forward with any of the design suggestions Evan and his fellow caller offered.

Knowing their ignored suggestions were good ones, Evan and his fellow caller reminded themselves they were both attending a business school. They pulled the trigger and decided to start their own goose call brand. When his fellow caller informed Evan he had access to a hot end lathe, the perfect tool to make the flutes, they saw the pieces of their small business coming together. Both felt they knew enough about the basic form of the flute to design a top-end call of their own.

Evan was committed to their new business adventure so as soon as he got off work, he would start creating, experimenting, and prototyping their designs. Evan built up a website and networked with apparel companies to brand their new business. Using their call for new competitions, Evan and his fellow caller continued to excel. They went on to win more call competitions, including a Minnesota state title. Just as their business and the call competitions were gaining momentum, an article about the accusations and subsequent charges at the lodge was published in the local newspaper and Evan's name was listed in the article.

Within hours, Evan's good name was being disparaged on various hunting websites, and Evan's business associate was getting nervous he would bring bad publicity to their fledgling startup. Even after Evan showed his fellow caller public statements from companies in support of him, it was not enough to convince his fellow caller. Evan and his business associate anxiously bantered back and forth over the collateral damage of negative media hype.

In the end, Evan knew their small business adventure was not based on a life-long friendship. He could not imagine himself working side by side with his fellow caller or see their small company, as it existed, grow, and flourish. Just like the waterfowl guide job, it was the end of another dream. Evan sadly realized; it was time to step aside. In his caller's heart, Evan eventually found peace because he knew he had been fully committed to the business from the beginning. Evan could not predict what the future held but God had a reason for the life lessons he had learned at the lodge and with his fellow goose caller. God also knew if Evan had stayed there and been too consumed in a goose calling business never destined to take flight, Evan would never have met his future soul mate.

Evan Catches His Future Wife

As one door closed, Evan found himself back in Grand Forks. As the summer was approaching, Evan was looking to shift gears and find a softball team to play on. Most summers he would land on some men's softball team, but after his abrupt move to Grand Forks, he had not found one to play on. Evan must have mentioned at his new workplace that he was looking to play, when a coworker told him, one of their regular guys was moving away and they needed another good player. His coworker warned him, this team had been together for a long, long time.

With the first game of the season, Evan wanted the regulars to know softball was not his first rodeo, so he showed up to play some serious ball in his baseball pants and jersey. The acting coach put Evan in leftfield. From his standpoint, Evan could see people arriving. Assuming they were loyal fans, he saw them staking out their usual positions to watch the game. Partway through the fourth inning, Evan starts to hear some mocking chants from a group of women, especially one, shouting out, "Hey New Guy, Who are You?" At the end of the inning, as Evan is running in, he hears her taunting voice again, "Hey New Guy, we don't let anyone join this team. You need to earn your spot. You look like a toddler, New Guy."

In the next inning, Evan was able to pull off a few superb plays. The first out was a diving catch. The second out was an easy infield fly ball. The spectacular third out came after he scooped up a fastball, turned his body in midair, and threw a straight shot to the second basemen. All three outs of that inning were impressively executed by Evan. At the top of the next inning, Evan was second at-bat and hit an inside the park homerun that rolled right up to the fence. As Evan crossed home plate and strutted by the group of women, he turned to his most sarcastic fan and proudly declared, "How was that for the New Guy? By the way, my name is Evan, not the New Guy!" He waited for her to reply, but there was silence. He saw and heard a cluster of the ladies murmuring loudly among themselves in astonishment. The "Comeback Queen" had no words, no rebuttal.

After the game, Evan was checking with the rest of his teammates about plans for the evening. He learned that the guys usually went to the team's sponsor bar and then moved off to another establishment, where the girls usually met up with the team later. At the next place, Evan went up to the bar to buy a round of drinks for his teammates. When he returned, he noticed one of the girls sitting at the table was "kinda cute." After an exchange of a few pleasantries, she looked at Evan and said, "You have no clue who I am, do you?" It hit Evan like a ton of bricks, he was casually talking to his tauntress, whom he nicknamed, "Sunglasses."

He did not recognize her with her hair down, all dressed up and looking "really cute." According to their close friends who witnessed their meeting firsthand, no one else mattered for the rest of the night. The new duo moved with the group, but Evan and Danielle did not talk to anyone else. They only had eyes for each other.

Like his old man, Evan admitted, he had a feeling immediately Danielle might be the one. Unlike his old man, Evan did not propose after two short weeks of dating. Their summer evenings were filled with softball games and other nights to get to know each other better. Evan was a little cautious at the beginning of their summer romance, too much reflection on unhappy, awkward endings with previous girlfriends. But with each date, Evan continued to sense Danielle could be his future wife.

His absolute tell-tale moment came when Evan had congregated with Danielle and many of her relatives at a family gathering near Concordia College. He was watching how Danielle was interacting with her mom, her dad, her sister, and all the rest of her relatives. These scenarios felt extremely familiar to him, just like the times he spent with us on Big Cormorant Lake with all the Sielings or his pal Pat, and the Wards. Chatting, eating, swapping jokes, laughing, sharing stories, and drinking some beers, it all felt incredibly comfortable.

Danielle's family had planned a cruise to Jamaica that winter and asked Evan to join them. Prior to leaving the port, Evan let Deb and I know that he had purchased a ring and planned to propose on the cruise. He had researched a few of the excursions offered on the trip, finding one he thought looked promising, near a waterfall. After talking with the concierge and other members of the crew he realized his first plan would be crushed when the Captain announced inclement weather was imminent. Knowing he could not propose without seeking approval from Danielle's parents, Evan found a moment to tell Dave and Lavonne of his new plans during a romantic dinner for two. Like most mischievous fathers, Dave made Evan squirm for a few agonizing minutes, but in the end, he gave Evan his blessing.

Plan B

Next, Evan talked with the concierge and the maître d' to find out the best way to propose at dinner. They suggested bringing out the ring on the dessert tray right after the meal. Many had tried and many had blissfully succeeded. Evan agreed to give their suggestion a solid try. During the dinner, Danielle felt like everyone on the staff was staring at her, so she was not enjoying her meal. Evan excused himself and went to look for the maître d' or any of the wait staff to sneak the ring to. He could not find anyone he had talked to earlier. So, when they finally brought out the dessert tray with no ring, it was super awkward and extremely anticlimactic. Evan was running out of time and he knew he had to do something. The plan he had shared with the folks was that after they left the dinner, ring on finger, they would meet Danielle's parents on another deck. He was familiar with the location of the meetup site and knew where the elevator would open and there would be her parents. Her mom would probably run up to her and scream congratulations. He knew he had to get this ring on her finger and fast.

The night was cold, rainy, and windy, but Evan suggested they step outside to go for a walk. Evan tried to make the moment more memorable by saying, "Just trust me. Do you trust me? Will you trust me for the rest of your life? as he presented a ring on his bended knee. "Yes! Yes!" Danielle chatters, "Can we please go inside now?" Evan could tell immediately the proposal went horribly wrong as they headed down to meet up site. In the elevator, Danielle started crying. Evan assumed it was not because she was so excited about getting an engagement ring. Before the elevator door opened, Danielle sighed, "I just didn't want my marriage proposal to go this way." As her mom dashed forward, embracing her in a huge hug, Danielle looked over at Evan and smiled, "Oh, okay, I get why you had to rush." Evan knew too, no other words needed to be spoken. To internally sense how a spouse feels, to have that flash of insight, an unspoken awareness can prove to be extremely valuable. There will come a time in the extremely near future when Danielle will sense, she needs to give Evan a critical assist.

A Triple Play

First, you need a little backstory. In the summer of Evan's sophomore year, Miranda was working at the Dairy Queen, and Deb and I had decided our kids were old enough so that we could leave for the weekend to attend a wedding. It would be the first time we would "leave all the kids home alone." In the afternoon Miranda decided to drive Evan and her friends to the Hutchinson Mall. As they were driving home, coming around the curve into Biscay, Evan had his hand out the opened window, undulating his hand up and down like a rolling wave in the wind. He remembered something hitting his hand like a rock and quickly pulling it inside only to find a bee flitting around and hanging on the side of his hand. Evan was surprised the bee was still attached by his stinger, so he flicked it off his hand, out the window, thinking, "Man, that really hurt."

The group stopped at the Dairy Queen to get a little free ice cream. As Evan started eating his frozen treat, he started feeling more and more uncomfortable and most importantly, itchy. After he and Miranda arrived home, Evan went into the bathroom and pulled up his shirt. and saw his whole torso along with his arms were covered in red raised patches or hives. Evan called Miranda into the bathroom to show her. Evan told her he thought he might be allergic to the peanuts in the Buster Parfait, but he wasn't sure. Miranda tried to stay calm and called a neighbor who lived a few houses down, Brad, a volunteer fireman. Luckily, Brad Morris answered the phone and was at our house in a matter of minutes.

Evan remembers standing on the porch as Brad parked his car and started walking up the sidewalk to our house. Brad did not make it to the porch before he took one look at Evan and could see he was struggling and announced, "We are going to the Emergency Room now." There are only a few other things Evan recalls because he fainted as soon as he got in Brad's car. Evan remembers Miranda crying, Brad in a dispute with a nurse about insurance, and shouting, "He is dying." He had a few more scattered memories of waking up in a bed, wearing a gown, and puking a few times, all while going in and out of consciousness. After his first strike, Evan was gifted with an epi-pen, a lifesaving injection. Evan would always need to carry one with him just in case he might have another allergic reaction to a bee sting.

Years later, my brother had invited Evan to go hunting with him. I really appreciated the fact that my older brothers made sure he was included in their fall hunting trips. On this trip, my brother brought Evan to his pal, Pat's house, near Fergus Falls. Pat's family including his cousins were all there. Evan, Pat, and some other guys were playing football in the front yard. Evan had attempted a diving catch and landed hands first in a pile of dead leaves. As he pulled his hand out, he saw a bee attached to his wrist. Knowing this was serious, Evan had attempted to keep his breathing regular as he tried to locate Pat's Mom or Dad to tell them he did not have his epi-pen with him and needed to alert his parents.

When we got the call from Susan, Pat's mom, she eagerly related Evan had been stung by a bee. My first question, "Does he have his epi-pen, and did he use it?" Her factual response, "No!" and "No!" Susan did convey that Evan was icing the site of the stinger, and she thought he was doing okay. As I was explaining the importance of getting Evan to a hospital, getting him checked over, getting an injection, Susan turned to look at Evan and realized he looked paler than he did minutes before. Evan has some vivid memories of Susan and I talking back and forth; Susan driving exceedingly fast and him feeling more and more lethargic in the back seat.

When my brother showed up at Susan and Pat's house to bring Evan his duffle bag, the bag that held his epi-pen, those still at the house told him Evan was in the ER. In true hunter fashion, my brother arrived at the Emergency Room in full camouflage. Evan's first question, feeling much better after an injection, "Can we still go hunting tomorrow?" Not even a second strike from this bee could stop Evan from thinking about hunting.

Years passed, and Evan had managed to stay clear of stinging insects. He was a few days away from his wedding and was outside taking the cover off the grill to prepare a little lunch for his fiancé. Danielle was on her way home to have lunch with him, an expected afternoon routine. When she came through the door, she called out his name. Danielle already thought it was unusual Evan had not responded to her text, *"On my way home for lunch."* When Evan came around the corner, she was surprised to see an awfully pale looking guy with an epi-pen in his hand. Evan was a wee bit proud of himself, this time he actually had his epi-pen. He was contemplating whether to stick himself. In his mind, Evan was envisioning an exceptionally large needle, Danielle very calmly said, "Evan you are going to go ahead and inject yourself with that pen. I am going to go get some crackers because I have not had lunch, then we are going to the ER. On the way, I am going to call your mom."

Evan followed Danielle's lead. Just as instructed, Evan jabbed the pen in his leg. The action was so quick, he never felt the needle. By the time they reached the hospital, Evan was already feeling better. The third strike of the bees had no power over Evan. With Danielle in his life, Evan, and his bride-to-be, handled the incident swiftly and calmly. As we hung up from her call, we remember saying to Danielle, "Thank you for taking care of Evan, for sicker or poorer, welcome to the family!"

A Working Man for All Seasons

In order to make your way in the world, boys need money. Boys need to work. Evan had wants and needs, so we suggested he get a job. I had grown up working on the farm but took my first job at sixteen when I could drive to work. But, if you are thirteen, almost fourteen, you want to earn some cash because you think you need a Country Club membership, you find a job delivering Saturday papers. With his first employment adventure, this meant Dad and son, got up early, got the papers, brought them home, folded them, bagged them, then finally delivered them. If you are involved in weekend sports in any way — like Evan was — then sometimes his first job became another part-time job for Dad. So, newspaper deliveries did not last long. But, for the record books, it was Evan's first paycheck.

Evan's second job was at Burger King. As a minor you had to work in front; you had to wait until you were sixteen before you got the glorious job of flipping burgers and wearing the black shirt, not the RED one that says, "Minor Working Here." The next set of jobs included the Pizza Ranch, the Glencoe Golf Course, Big 5 Sporting Goods, Sears, Walmart, Hunting Guide, TGIF, Hooligans, Buffalo Wild Wings, Digi-Key Electronics, back to Buffalo Wild Wings, the Tavern, Sofa Mart, Wells Fargo, Shields and driving trucks to haul earth. With each job, lessons were learned, skills were acquired, relationships were strengthened, and most importantly several connections were made.

What Danielle knew about Evan was that it did not matter what job he held, if Evan struck up a conversation with anyone, both parties walked away thinking they would be friends for life. She told Evan, "You are a people person, you are not confrontational, and folks just love you. When you were a guide, you could chat with a farmer, and within five minutes, he would agree to let you hunt on his land." In Grand Forks, the story goes, you either farm, you work for the family farm, you know somebody who farms, or you sell products that farmers need.

In this farm community, Danielle was certain Evan could land a steady job; a job where he could make a living utilizing his easy-going conversational skills of bantering with farmers. While hauling dirt, and being an Ice Road Trucker, Evan started researching companies selling primarily to farmers. There was one company that caught his interest, CHS, and they were looking for truckers. Evan continued to dig deeper into this global agribusiness owned by farmers, ranchers, and cooperatives across the United States. He noticed CHS was a big company with big integrity. What he used to tell me, his dad, a guy who grew up on a farm, ". . . CHS does a ton of great things, and farmers are cool because farming feeds the world. Corn, wheat, soybeans, or whatever you raise on farms can be distributed around the globe. It could be extremely impactful to work for a company that feeds the world." My son was on fire for CHS.

While helping Danielle out at the clothing store where she worked, Evan met a customer one day. During some small talk, he found out the customer worked for CHS. Evan enthusiastically told this guy he wanted to apply for an internship with CHS. The customer inquired about Evan's age and his thinking process on starting out with an internship. As Evan explained, "I want to understand as much as I can about farming. I am not an agronomist, so I need a summer to learn a little more." The customer quizzed Evan further, "What is your background experience?"

Evan replied, "Well, I have a broad background in computers, technology, and software. I can build websites. I have had a ton of sales experience. A ton, and I was a key player in a small start-up business." The CHS employee looked at Evan and declared, "Evan, I want you to send me your resumé. We are looking for people who understand technology, who can speak to farmers, and can make technology make sense to farmers. We call this position a yield-point specialist." Evan got the CHS guy's email and went back to work.

The CHS guy, who knew Danielle from previous shopping, told her, "I think I am going to hire your husband. I hope that is okay." Danielle hastily responded, "Yes, in fact, you can take him now."

You Did Not Know Dirt

A year later at CHS, as one of the newest members of the yield-point team, Evan was teaching an intern how to write fertility equations using one of the satellite maps from the precision agriculture services team. A general manager walked by and inquired what the two of them were doing. Evan looked up and explained himself. The GM smiled at Evan and affirmed, "When we hired you, you didn't know dirt about farming, and now you are explaining fertility equations to our interns!" Evan smiled back, "It's simple math." The GM smirked, "And, that's why we hired you, Evan."

Evan contemplates if having your father be an educator for forty years, or a mom running in-home daycare for thirteen years, or both of them being foster parents for fifteen years, has helped him learn anything, it is how being a member of a family and a community is not always about you. Providing a service, giving back, or answering God's calling determines the actions that make your life full. Understanding God's timing and God's plan for him have has sometimes been incredibly hard lessons to learn. In the end, Evan has come out a better person for going through these journeys and fully understanding that God had orchestrated each high point and each low point to bring him and Danielle together.

I attribute some of our children's life lessons could be a little smoother if we borrow a parenting sports analogy from our local pastor. Having a son who is passionate about sports and hunting, we found these approaches are always relevant and valuable. If you can switch back and forth between three different roles as a parent, you can adapt to whatever the situation calls for.

Deb and I first heard this sports analogy in a sermon. In the first proactive role, you may want to act as a Groundskeeper. In this role, you mark out and clearly explain the boundaries. You fully explain what is expected and what is allowed. In a second position, you may find the need to act as a Referee. Your primary job in this role is to call out the fouls of wrongful or hurtful behaviors, while enforcing the penalties if corrections need to be made or consequences need to be imposed. The third role, the one I cherish the most, is that of a Coach. A good Coach needs to be aware and alert to those teachable moments. To help prepare your children for the game of life instead of benching them to keep them safe. Our advice is to use these approaches interchangeably; you monitor and adjust; you pivot with each set of circumstances. What we have learned more than anything; parenting is not about a formula for perfection, but a path of faithfulness.

My preferred teachable moments with Evan are to answer a question with another probing question. If you ever find yourself in a situation where you need to gather more data before you can make the most informed decision, or deal out the most logical consequence, answer your child's question with another incisive question.

Evan has shared the teaching gene has come to the surface a few times in his role as a manager. To learn as much as he can in a limited time about his fellow employees, Evan answers their inquiries by asking more insightful questions. When Evan believes he has heard all he needs to render a resolution, he is able to present a satisfying solution which usually ensures everyone's voice is being heard.

In the end, whether you are nurturing your child, or building up a colleague, the heart of parenting, starts in the heart of the parent. But no parenting strategy, no practical method, no sports analogy could adequately prepare us for what lay ahead with the birth of Miranda and Evan's little sister, Abby Justine.

7

STRONG & COURAGEOUS

When you are a schoolteacher in the Midwest, you have those three infamous months to be at home with your family for the summer. So, when Deb informed me that she was pregnant again, we did the calculations and we figured out our third baby was coming in July. I was happy because this meant I did not have to request sick days or personal days when our baby arrived. You genuinely get one glorious month of paternity leave to enjoy your new baby bundle before school resumes after Labor Day. The timing had worked perfectly for us with Evan. After visiting the doctor, we were a bit amazed this due date was so similar to another one. Evan's birthday was July 28, and baby number three was due to arrive around the same day.

Miranda's labor was long, and Evan's was even longer. As we moved into June, with two kids at home, our doctor suggested we have Deb induced and pick the day for baby number three. Summer is time for you to make big plans, like a vacation to Disney World, Yellowstone, or big decisions like when do you want the birth of your final biological baby? We had made another big decision for the summer as well. In the doctor's office, I was explaining my scheduled procedure for July. Our doctor's immediate response was to reconsider. His position was clear, "You are both so young . . . if something were to happen, don't you want that door to stay open, so you could try again?" Deb and I assured him, the plans for my vasectomy were already in motion and we trusted God had everything in control. Her previous pregnancies had been without any complications, why would we worry now? We thanked him for his concern and settled on July 24 for the arrival of baby number three.

Our Triple Coincidence

This may not be a significant claim to fame for some, but we thought the circumstances were something incredibly unique. After Deb was induced and we were in our labor delivery room, we realized it was the same hospital room both Miranda and Evan had been born in. The same doctor, the same room, it all had to be a sign that everything with this birth was going to be okay. What we did not know, because we just did not ask, is that induced labor is a wee-bit more intense. The contractions came on suddenly and forcefully. The drugs they used must induce chatting as well. I distinctly remember our doctor telling Deb to stop talking and push. A few minutes later, Abby Justine Sieling, our sweet, beautiful girl, entered the world loudly on July 24, 1985. Something else was also unique besides the same room, the same doctor, all three of our babies were 8 pounds 3 ounces, and nineteen inches long. Not sure if other families experienced the same height and weight phenomena, but the final event did not end there. It was already a long hot, humid summer; Deb found herself in the hallway, with newborn, Abby, and a pillow on her lap, and me in the basement during another Tornado Warning, just like we had with Evan. Deb and Abby came home from the hospital on July 28th. Our family of five felt complete as we stopped to buy Evan a McDonald's birthday cake for his second birthday.

Life in Rothsay stayed exceptionally busy raising three young children of our own and operating a thriving daycare, all located in the same house. Deb had developed a close friendship, and later a partnership, with the wife of one of my school colleagues. Her name was Cindy, and she agreed to teach the morning preschool in the daycare. Depending on the needs of the families, they might bring their wee ones two or three mornings a week to the preschool, with most of the kiddos staying the rest of the afternoon in the daycare. Just like Evan and Miranda, Abby's friendships were made as new families came and went through the years in the preschool and the daycare. Abby herself attended the preschool three days a week when she was old enough, with Cindy as her teacher. In the afternoons, Abby became Cindy's best baby helper; bringing diapers, wet wipes, or something from a diaper bag as requested by either Cindy or Deb. If asked to help in any way, Abby was ready and able. Abby loved doting over the new babies, and she loved helping Cindy more.

Mom, You Ran Over Me!

Even at the age of four, on many occasions, Abby was not only asserting herself as daycare helper extraordinaire, but she was also letting her mom know she preferred all outcomes end in her favor. For instance, one day when Deb discovered the daycare was out of milk, Abby insisted she should ride along. Such an opportunity could easily end in a special treat while she and her mom were at the store. The Tiger Mart, the only grocery store in town was only a few blocks away. Deb was already weary of her incessant begging and conceded to her request to ride along.

Deb and I had owned a few older cars in high school and attending college. We were ready when we finally purchased our first new car right off the lot, a red Pontiac 1000 hatch-back. As a subcompact, resembling a Chevy Chevette, it was just the right size to transport the two adults in the front and our trio in the back. It was enough of a sweet treat to sit in the front by mom, who had finally agreed because she needed to get back to the daycare with the milk. As Deb turned into our driveway, she did not see Abby had a grip on the door handle. The momentum of the turning car, as well as the extra weight of a four-year-old leaning against the door, was too much of a combination as the passenger side door swung open, and Abby slipped out of sight. In that moment, what does a parent do? Come to an immediate stop. What if her child had slipped under the car? Do you keep going, hoping between the speed of the moving vehicle, the force of the swinging door, and the weight of your child were all enough to throw her free of the car and pray she landed safely on the lawn? Before other worrisome thoughts entered her mind, Deb felt the car roll over something, and she froze. She closed her eyes. Deb did not want to get out of the car for fearing what she might find. Suddenly, Abby pops up in the frame of the opened door, with both hands on her hips. Abby immediately shouted at her mother, "You ran over me!" When Deb has retold this story over the years, and she has told it many times, she always reminds herself, "On that day, I was never so happy to have Abby yell at me."

Deb quickly put the car in park, turned the key, and flew out of her seat. She ran to the other side of the car and picked up Abby in her arms and hurried down the stairs to the daycare, shouting for Cindy to come quick. Deb was too nervous and afraid to even look. After she explained what happened, Deb asked Cindy to assess Abby. Cindy put Abby on her lap and thoroughly examined her arms, hands, torso, stomach, legs, and feet. All they found across the back of both calves, were two sets of distinct tire marks. Abby must have fallen out of the car, landing on the grass. When a harried Deb took too wide of a turn, the door flew open, sending Abby out the opened door. Deb released her foot from the gas pedal, yet the momentum of the car rolled over Abby's legs before coming to a stop. After a thorough check, Cindy determined Abby was physically okay. Once the shock wore off, both Deb and Abby showed no lingering signs of the trauma. To this day, this family folklore incident has been christened, "The day Mom drove over Abby".

The "running over my daughter with the family car" incident happened while we were living in the "white house" near the city park. Most of Abby's childhood memories are centered around the white house. It was a three-bedroom rambler with a full basement. Mom and Dad had the biggest bedroom. Miranda had her own, and Evan and Abby shared the third bedroom. To keep them both happy, we split the room down the middle and painted two walls pink and two walls blue. Deb stitched a quilt with pink geometric and floral designs for Abby's twin bed and a sports-themed quilt with a mixed palette of blues for Evan. If Evan and Abby were not together in their shared bedroom, they were busy outside playing on the swing set-slide-fort Deb's dad, Sonny, had built for the family. One of their favorite inventions for the back yard was a combination of an old Wonder Rocking Horse aluminum frame where a smashed resin horse had been removed, with a Schwinn Banana bicycle seat that was attached to the big metal springs. Both Miranda and Evan recall numerous adventures in the back yard with the fort, the apple tree, and the Wonder Banana Rocker.

Double Trouble

Sometimes, Abby and Evan played well together and were thick as thieves. Sometimes, Evan would follow Abby around the yard kneeing her in the back and act like an awful big brother. Other times they would join forces; partaking in mischief together, knowing trouble from one of their parents was soon headed their way. After we moved into the white house, I had converted the empty basement into a full-sized bathroom and a large L-shaped room running the length of the house with a nice drop ceiling for Deb's daycare. Along one wall, we installed a set of hanging kitchen cupboards and lower cabinets for games, toys, and arts & crafts storage.

One of the more enjoyable craft items were some colored liquid soaps Deb or Cindy would squirt on the tabletop as the kids used wet sponges to clean and polish the long table. Abby and Evan enjoyed working with the colored soap so much, they took it upon themselves to spread the neon-colored liquid all over the table, the chairs the lower cabinets, and the walls. When Deb discovered their creative mess, she demanded Abby and Evan help with the cleanup. When Abby started to protest, she gave Abby a good swat across her bottom. Abby immediately ran up the stairs crying and waited at the top for Evan to follow. She heard her mom give Evan a good smack across his bottom as well. However, Evan did not start crying. Just the opposite, he started laughing. This only made Deb more frustrated with the whole nasty spectacle, so she swatted Evan again. Evan came running up the stairs, holding his backside. The two little Picassos both ran to their room and hid out, far away from their mom for the rest of the day. Thick as thieves and two times the trouble.

Abby was more than ready to start Kindergarten when she turned five. Even with a late July birthday, Abby made the cut-off, and she trotted off to start her education. Her favorite memory of our favored Kindergarten teacher, Mrs. Eklund, was the class Teddy Bear. Each week, one lucky student was able to take the class Teddy home for the weekend. Their special class friend had his own diary to write about your home adventures, share family photos, and a travel bag of clothes to dress him up during the weekend. Abby could not wait until it was her time to be chosen to bring home Teddy. The wait was worth it according to Abby, because his visit to our house did not disappoint. Abby treated him like a real baby during his stay; making sure Teddy was fed, changed, read to, played with, and entertained for thirty straight hours. Her "Mama's Little Helper" genetic code was in full swing.

Abby was truly a caregiver at heart. Unfortunately, her big heart may have happened to be her demise in first grade. Abby would sometimes complain to Deb she thought her teacher was not always kind to her classmates. This made Abby's heart sad and she chose to avoid any opportunities to witness this. Many mornings, she would beg her mother to let her stay home from school. One morning she was so adamant about not going, she held tightly onto the doorknob and refused to leave the house. Deb literally had to peel her little fingers off the knob, while nudging her out the door with her legs and then promptly closing and locking the door with Abby on the other side. Abby banged on the door for a few minutes, begging to stay home until she realized Deb was not going to let her come back in. Mercifully, we only lived a few blocks from the school, so Deb gave it a few minutes then called one of the ladies in the front office to make sure Abby had finally arrived at school. Abby continued to struggle with first grade, but she mustered through and made it to second grade which revitalized her love for school again. Her teacher happened to be the mother of one of her best friends in the daycare. Abby was well acquainted with Rachel's mom and could not wait to have Mrs. Thysell, as her teacher. Abby had already experienced some home playdates and a couple of sleepovers at her second-grade teacher's house. For Abby, second grade was an amazing year.

Like her brother and sister, Abby had a collection of Elementary school friends. With some who lived out in the country, it was more difficult to plan outings with them. Those in town, especially those within walking distance, had optimal benefits. One of her good friends lived next to the school football field. In the fall, during the football season, the action off the field was much more fun than watching the home games. In the winter, the hill flanking the field was perfect for sliding.

When the ice-skating rink opened near the field at the bottom of the hill, Abby spent endless hours with friends. Reminiscing about sitting on the hill, with a pack of candy cigarettes, pretending their frozen breath looked exactly like exhaled smoke brings on giggles even today.

Other events elicit smiles; especially when you think of the time you spend with the same kids and teacher for one hundred and eighty days. Class parties, group projects, rowdy recesses, cafeteria hijinks, prepping for assignments, quizzes, and tests. . . the list goes on and on. For Abby, another cherished memory was the fact she and Evan had the chance to eat out at a Pizza Hut with her third-grade teacher, Mrs. Walter, and then got to hang out at her house while her thankful parents were off attending some family event. It surprises me which memories stick and which ones we try to forget. For example, in fourth grade, Abby was not too fond of her teacher. She recalls an argument with him, which resulted in her being sent to the principal's office. Even though Abby cannot pinpoint the exact context of the argument, she knows she was mad at him. Abby was told to go to the office, and the principal said she had to sit there until she could say she was sorry. Stubborn Abby remembers sitting there for an exceptionally long time. In the end, her fourth-grade teacher redeemed himself when he introduced her to the world of word searches. He used hundreds of these pages as his primary busy work. Abby fell in love with word searches back then and loves doing them to this day. In fifth grade, she had the same teacher, that Miranda and Evan had, Mrs. Brandt. She just so happened to be one of her dad's best friends, so Abby tried really hard not to get into any trouble that year. She did kiss her first boy in fifth grade but swears it was only on the cheek.

With the start of sixth grade, Abby was destined to fall into the same ranks as Evan and Miranda; a full school year with her dad as her teacher. Alas, this was the summer we packed up and left Rothsay after sixteen years and moved to

Glencoe, Minnesota. Abby would not have me as her sixth-grade teacher. Before the move, I had secured a job as one of the fourth-grade teachers at their local elementary school. Abby tells me, she always resented the fact I was not her sixth-grade teacher. Looking back, this missing piece of her childhood may have been the catalyst for issues to come.

Moving to a new town, invites countless challenges; new classmates, new teachers, the potential for new friends, and hopefully new positive experiences. For most, a move could be a new beginning. A time of hope and happiness. We do not believe that was the path Abby was on. She immediately felt intimated by all these new changes. Glencoe's school was ten times bigger than Rothsay's and the first strike was not having a single homeroom teacher. All the sixth graders shared the group of teachers specializing in different subject areas. What was supposed to be a great preparation to switch for each class period, just like high school, was a bit overwhelming for Abby. She did make some plausible connections with a few of her peers, mostly because they shared the same teachers, or held the same interest in sports. Some connections were stronger than others. Rollerblading, jumping on trampolines, bonfires, backyard camping, and visiting at classmates' houses after home football games did manage to fill up her social life. What was different for Abby, she kept these girls at a distance. They were her peers, her girls, her classmates, yet were not those deep-rooted relationships like her brother's and sister's forever friends. Not all her friends were girls. With a town ten times the size of Rothsay, there was far more male fish in this pond and Abby had her sights on a school of them.

As her parents, based on previous practices with Abby's siblings, we set boundaries as we had done before. We asked numerous questions; we confirmed plans, addresses, phone numbers, and we tried to verify with unfamiliar parents what we were hearing from Abby was accurate and honest. The difference in Rothsay, we knew the families and parents for sixteen years. Trust had been built and earned over time. In Glencoe, we only knew what our children told us. Sometimes we learned more about other parents through our peers at work. As some parents checked out, you start to widen your trust circle, hoping and praying your child could make good choices. Sadly, if curfews are broken, you catch a lingering whiff of cigarette smoke or the distinct odor of alcohol, the trust circle shrinks. When it comes down to it, you want to trust your child to make good choices, or at least you believe their actions feel like the right choice.

The town of Silver Lake was part of the Glencoe school district our children were attending. Silver Lake was more comparable to Rothsay in terms of city size and population. Like Rothsay, they also had their traditional city-wide happenings and celebrations. One, in particular, was the well-known Pola-Czesky Days. This three-day observance for the town of Silver Lake began in 1955. We learned that event has been known by a variety of names including Silver Lake Family Days, Silver Lake's Carnival Funfest and Appreciation Days, and Pole-Czech Community Festival Days. Around 1972, their hometown festival finally became Pola-Czesky Days. Their weekend festival featured kickball tournaments, toilet bowl races, mini tractor pulls, kiddie parades, a polka mass, fireworks, and dances with live music. It was during these celebratory days that Abby admits she began dabbling in partying, drinking, and smoking marijuana. Abby dabbled so well during Pola-Czesky Days, she has an extremely clear recollection of a fellow volleyball player sticking her long fingers down her throat to induce vomiting because the girl was too nervous about Abby and possible alcohol poisoning.

It was a good thing some of Abby's teammates became her protectors at these parties because there were more parties. To tell the truth, sports became a place for Abby to shine because of the God-given athletic skills and talents she had been blessed with. In middle school, she played volleyball in the fall, gymnastics in the winter, and softball and later track in the spring. Abby was a powerful player in any sport she chose to participate in. The force behind her volleyball spikes could knock an opponent off her feet. On the springboard in gymnastics, she advanced quickly, and made the varsity team, and was developing a name for herself on the floor and the vault. Abby was clearly not in the shadow of her big sister.

We do joke about her efforts on the softball diamond. Since her brother, Evan loved this sport, we assumed Abby might replicate his passion. As she reminisces about the game, she could throw the ball as hard as anyone else, run the bases faster than the other girls, and if she played catcher or short-stop, she could take a ball to the face and play on. What her parents remember was a bleached blonde girl standing near second base waiting for a ball to come her way with the most disgusted look they had ever seen on her face. When the inning was over, with no action near her, we overheard Abby say to the members of her team kicking dirt as she stomped towards the dugout, "Who in the hell would want to play this stupid game? You stand there all day — waiting and waiting for someone to hit a ball your way. It's hot, it's boring, who in their right mind would invent such a ridiculous game!"

When we moved to Chandler, Arizona, Abby was a Junior, and once again, sports were her safety net. A place to feel noticed and define herself. In Arizona, fall sports fans do not require winter coats, stocking caps, or warm gloves. A few of the locals, who had either acclimated to the weather or lived there all their lives, brought portable gas heaters to the soccer games. Deb and I just shook our heads with sheer delight because we were wearing shorts and sandals in the bleachers in October. In most Arizona schools, volleyball is considered a winter sport, so Abby just decided to be a walk-on for soccer tryouts. She had never played the game, but with her muscular gymnastic legs, when she made contact, the ball rocketed down the field with lightning speed. At some of the home games, Deb and I heard the mutterings of some of the long-standing locals complaining about how the new girl had taken a spot from a varsity player. It was a similar story for track in the Spring. Abby had never thrown shot put before, but with her awesome arms, she went to State by the end of her first season.

As a high schooler in Chandler, Abby was in the same situation as Evan. She was ahead in required credits, allowing her to end her day at noon and take a job. Abby found employment with an excellent real estate company in Chandler who provided a passion and an incentive for her to pursue a career after graduating from high school in 2003. Chandler was an up and coming suburb in Arizona. There were more kids in Abby's graduating class than the entire town of Rothsay. I missed the old days of a smaller town when my teacher friends would shuffle through our graduation announcements and determine which Senior had invited us to their homes to celebrate their accomplishment. If one of my best friends, Joan, and I had the same invites, we would travel in and out of the festivities together. If Joan had a name and I did not, I would wait in the car, while she dropped off her card, make the rounds, and then off to the next graduation party we would go. We would repeat the same practice in reverse if I had an invite from one of my speech students or thespians. Joan and I would save the same invites for a later time where we would end the evening of celebrations.

In Arizona, in an exceptionally large high school, one you have only attended for two years, an afternoon of party hopping was simply not going to happen. Abby chose to celebrate with two friends at a local restaurant where they tried out such delicacies as south mountain nachos, cheesy jalapeño bacon macaroni, and authentic rattlesnake.

Empty Nesters

After graduation, Abby was itching to move out of our three-bedroom home with a pool, for an apartment of her own. She had been working with the real estate firm for some time and had made her first big purchase; a little blue Chevy Cavalier, 2 Door Coupe. We tried to instill in Abby, living on your own, or even with a roommate, means maintaining fiscal responsibility and a strict budget. We did not say no, we said what we had learned worked best to answer Abby, we said, "Not Yet!" We gave her three months. In three months, if she had enough money saved for the standard amount required to rent an apartment, utilities if required, make her car payments, as well keep food on the table and gas in the tank, then and only then, we would say, "Now!". After three months, by sustaining a strict budget, Abby proved she was very capable of living on her own.

If living on her own had stayed the plan for a few more years, Abby's story may have written a different chapter. We could say with certainty, if Abby had never met the person she later married, her story would have changed. For the next few years, Abby was a top performer at work, a dedicated employee, a responsible young woman, and she kept her apartment immaculate. She liked to disinfect and clean like her dad. If at any time Abby felt like she was losing control of her life, she would try to take back the power by keeping her house in order. When she was younger, Abby used cleaning as a way to release tension and anger. You knew Abby was boiling underneath if you came into her room and the bed looked like no one had ever slept there, all her shoes were in a conspicuous row, toes pointing forward, paired together with mere centimeters between them. Just beware, Abby might be ready to explode.

Red Flags

We knew Abby was dating guys and she had been serious about a couple of them. Because she was always mature and professional around her mom and me, we did not question her day to day life. So, at age 23, we were taken by surprise when Abby told us she was pregnant, and she was planning to get married. According to the boy – the impregnator — if he and Abby got married this week, she could be on his insurance. They needed the insurance to pay the medical bills when her baby came. He had this all planned out, even down to the minute. He figured out, if everybody did what they were supposed to do during his lunch break, in and out with the Justice of the Peace, they could get back to work. If his scrupulous planning was not a red flag, with a preview of his self-centered behavior, then it was my fault for not seeing it sooner. He also encouraged Abby to get married while her mom was out of town.

We did not have the money at that time to pay for the change to Deb's plane ticket, so Miranda and I agreed to be their legally required witnesses. Miranda was very pregnant with her second child, Brayah, and I did not have anyone I trusted to babysit our foster daughter. So, Stephanie in her stroller and I, showed up at the Justice of the Peace and waited for Miranda to arrive. I had stopped at a local florist to purchase a small bouquet for Abby and a boutonniere for the groom. After Miranda waddled through the door, we walked up to the counter together, with me pushing a stroller. We made eye contact with the person behind the counter and told her we were here for a wedding. Her first look of contempt was obvious on her face, as she eyed Miranda's belly. A second look of disdain, to acknowledge there was an obvious age difference. With a third and finally glare of condescension, she peered over at the sleeping baby in the stroller. She clicked her tongue and stated, "Oh, I bet you are." Realizing what thoughts were racing through her dysfunctional brain, we quickly responded in unison, "Not us, my daughter, her sister is getting married today, and she told us to check-in at the desk to find out what room the ceremony would be in." After we provided Abby and the groom's full names, she gave us directions. It took longer to find the room than the actual ceremony. I took the wedding party to lunch at a nearby Texas Roadhouse and then the bride and the groom went back to work. Waiting for Deb to answer, to tell her about the day, another red flag, another alarm was going off in my head, "What did our baby girl just do?"

What my little girl did, was follow along with whatever this manipulator told her to do. We suspected that Abby was using drugs and drinking after high school. Like most parents, we hoped Abby had it all under control, and not the drugs and alcohol taking control over her. After the birth of their daughter in 2008, Abby became a poser. For a while, she could perform at her job, still get to work on time, and present herself as "all together" from 9 to 5. After work, she was drinking more, and more. Living with this negative influencer, Abby's drug and alcohol use took priority over her paying the bills. When she told us she was pregnant again, we were worried about their unborn baby because of the numerous experiences we had with our drug-exposed foster babies. Abby was harboring something else, something she would not share. There was an added tension, like someone had flipped a switch on their relationship. Even after their son was born healthy, we still saw more friction, and things at work were not going well for Abby either. Her after work-life had started drifting over into her day job and she was no longer a top performer. She was probably days away from getting fired when things flared up between the kid's dad and Deb.

To Deb, he came across as entitled and demanded that it was her responsibility, as the grandparent to help Abby and him out if he asked for it. As a result, Deb tried; she had talked to her brother who had bought a home in Arizona. Thankfully, he agreed to let Abby rent his home when they had to leave their apartment complex. Do not ask, it is complicated. When they did not pay the rent as they had promised, Deb's brother asked them to leave and the situation got volatile. Deb and Abby were disagreeing on any and all things when it came to the kids and the poor decisions they were making as a family. When grandpa and grandma in California said they had a trailer available for all four of them to move into, Abby agreed to leave Arizona. On the day of the move, the two babies were a mess.

Their children did not want to be left at our house while their parents were packing for the move. After hours of their hysterics, Deb called their dad and told them the kids had been upset since they left and would not stop crying. His response was an accusatory rant about Deb supposedly being this infamous child whisperer and the truth was, she could not take care of her own goddamn grandchildren. I had not agreed to help with the move in any way. As I was walking through the door after a day of work, I could hear this man-child screaming at my wife over the phone. I waved my arms and tried to get her attention. I insisted she hang up on him, but Big Red must have the last word. In a way, it really was the last word. Abby, her kids, and their dad, left Arizona a few hours later in January of 2011, and we did not speak in person again for several months.

I tried to maintain communication after their departure. For weeks, it was hit or miss. We would talk to Abby about the kids and we rarely asked about their dad. Abby first shared how his dad was helping them keep a budget, pay their bills, make sure the grandkids were always taken care of. Over time, his monitored assistance and ongoing financial support were somehow perceived as a burden. He was complaining they would be indebted to his parents. Because his parents had changed the way they were doing life before their son and his family moved back to San Diego, his complaints were unwarranted. Her parroted criticisms did not sound like the Abby who knew she should be grateful. The rants came across as mimicked grumblings, somehow a mirrored reflection of how her husband felt. For as long as we had known him, Abby's husband had always felt that people owe him; never did he need to earn it, or work for it. If you were not giving him a handout, he had little time for you. If you were not moving his agenda along, he would find someone else who would.

Deb, Our Girl is in Trouble

Something must have happened between them because the frequency of Abby's calls started to increase. She had a feeling in her gut; her husband had moved on and was cheating on her. In 2010, technology made it quite easy for Abby to confirm her suspicions. She created a fictitious Facebook page with stock image photos, links, and items similar to his interests, and tagged her husband. When a strange woman asked to friend her, already linked to her husband, Abby was able to follow her and found posted pictures of the woman and her husband, along with several comments and emoticons hinting they were much more than acquaintances with similar interests. After taking screenshots of her posts, Abby confronted him. Of course, he denied everything. Then, in typical narcissistic fashion, proceeded to blame Abby for all that was going wrong in his life, included having children. Abby was so lost, so hurt and so alone. She was struggling trying to keep her marriage together with a person who did not want to be with her. Abby could not control how she was feeling; she was losing an internal battle of hopelessness and loneliness. He did offer to take her to a hospital. He dropped her off at the entrance and drove away.

When Abby first suspected he was having an affair, she called me. She was sad, scared, worried, all the emotions that come with the realization your husband has not been faithful. She told me she had proof, screenshots that he could not explain away this time, and she would be confronting him in the next few days. We made an agreement that she would call me every afternoon on my way home from work. We did this every afternoon for a week until I did not hear from her for two days. When Abby did not respond to any texts or message, I decided to call his mother, a phone number I had asked Abby for earlier and put away in my contacts before the grandkids moved away. His mother answered after a few rings. I explained I was worried about Abby because I had not heard from her for two days. There was a long moment of silence before she spoke. Then his mother started, "He told me he already called you to tell you Abby was in the hospital."

You cannot imagine the thoughts racing through my head at the word "hospital." I imagined Abby had confronted him and he had hurt her. Or she had tried to hurt herself, or there had been a physical fight, and they had hurt each other. His mother set out to explain more. "My son is worried about the kids because of the way Abby is acting. He decided he would bring her to a hospital. He stayed with her, consulting with the doctor, and the three of them agreed Abby should check herself in for a psychological evaluation." When I asked for the address and the phone number of the hospital, she simply replied, she did not have either, and I would have to call him to get those. Before we hung up, his mom sweetly assured me that the kids were okay. She continued on, by reminding me her son was simply trying to protect their children from our daughter's hysterics. She ended the call by reiterating, "She loved her grandchildren and her son very much; this was a lot for all of them to go through. Perhaps it was best he and Abby had this time apart." I hung up the call and found Deb's number. I started the next call by saying, "Deb, our girl is in trouble."

My next call was to get the numbers and address of the hospital. It was a short call; no pleasantries were exchanged. I would not give him the opportunity to elaborate on his side of his story. That evening, we intentionally brought Miranda and

Evan into the conversations and Miranda and Deb decided to leave from Phoenix the next day, so they could be in San Diego in time for visiting hours at the Psychiatric hospital. We could only confirm a few things after reaching the hospital's front desk. We verified the exact address; Abby was a patient there, and visitors were only allowed for a 1-hour visit between 6 and 7 PM. It had been nine months since Deb and Miranda had seen Abby.

Once they signed in, they had to leave everything in a locker. Nothing that could be used as a weapon or instrument for self-harm could be in their possessions; it all had to be locked away. They were surprised to see how thin Abby was. Her high and low behaviors led them to believe she was going through some type of withdrawals. Once they started talking, they were not surprised to know her caretaker role had resurfaced, and Abby had already made friends with another patient she wanted to invite to Thanksgiving because she did not have a family in California. Deb and Miranda had arrived early enough to purchase some comfortable clothes, underwear, and bras for her. Abby was so excited and thankful someone thought enough about her to bring her new clothes. The hour went by quickly, so they made plans to see each other the next night during visiting hours. That next visit they talked a little more about her plans for when she would be released. It was apparent the thought of leaving the hospital left Abby agitated and even frightened. When Miranda and Deb left California, Deb knew she had to find a safe harbor, a shelter for her daughter as fast as she could.

After the 7 PM visit was over, Deb and Miranda drove through the night and arrived back in Arizona around 1 AM. As soon as she woke up, Deb started calling every rehabilitation facility she could find. She started with the most well-known and those easily located on the internet. Some were in Iowa, some good choices in Minnesota, and a few more in other states. Everyone she talked to needed some type of mental health insurance, or required twenty-five thousand dollars for a thirty-day stay. During her numerous conversations, she learned it would be best for Abby, legally, to stay in California. Deb zeroed her focus on California, faith-based rehabilitation facilities. She was excited when she talked to an angel named, George. He operated a state-funded group home offering a proven program, and wanted twenty-five hundred dollars for thirty days. The cost was definitely more affordable, but we did not have that type of disposable income. Deb reached out to her mom, Maxine, explaining all that had happened. Her gracious mom agreed to give us the money.

In her conversations with George, he advised and highly recommended based on his numerous success stories, that we offer Abby's potential time at the rehabilitative group home as a gift, not a demand. That would be easy because Maxine's generous offer would make that the truth. When Abby called to let us know that she was going to be released, Deb and I drove to San Diego and checked into a hotel room before we picked her up. We walked along the beach and told her how much we loved her, how much we wanted to grow old with her, watch her children grow up, and how much they both needed their mom. Then we offered her the gift of a thirty-day stay in this group home we found in Orange County. She did not accept the gift right away; she mulled it over for a day and a half before she finally agreed to go. Deb and I were so relieved that she was willing to commit to getting better, to stop drinking, to stop doing drugs, to rewrite her story.

As we prepared for her stay, together we pushed a grocery cart through a local grocery store with Abby in the middle and Deb and I on either side. We watched her hands tremble as we agreed on each item to place in the cart. After we helped her unbag her groceries and place them in the upper cabinets assigned to her, we had to say our goodbyes to Abby for thirty days. For the next thirty days, we could only talk to the house mom, not to our daughter. We could check on her progress, ask if she was attending all AA meetings, doing her house chores, eating well, but we could not talk to Abby. After hugging her tight, we stepped outside and walked towards our car. After we drove away, I pulled over to the side of the road, put the car in park, turned to Deb, and said, "What the hell did we just do?" We just left our daughter with strangers. We bought her some groceries, gave her a big hug, and said 'we'll see you again in thirty days.' We took twenty-five hundred dollars from your mother. We only had the words of a guy named George who promised he could help her; what the hell did we just do?"

What we did do was give Abby to God. We knew He had a plan for her because she was still alive. She had not succumbed totally to a darker world that she could not come back from. After her first thirty days, she let us know that she thought it would be best if she stayed for another thirty. We still did not have that kind of money, and we were not going to ask Deb's mom again. God showed us a way to find another twenty-five hundred dollars. You cannot put a price on your child's life, but five thousand dollars was the price we would gladly pay to keep our daughter alive and bring her safely home someday.

After two, thirty-day stays in the group home, the director and Abby agreed it was time for her to write the first chapter in her new story. When Abby was weeks away from being released, it was sinking in hard. What would she do when she had her children back? That was number one. Abby was really going to be alone; her support system from the home would be gone. That was number two. Her place of residence, with her soon to be ex-husband was gone. Oh yes, he made sure he filed for divorce before Abby began her first thirty days. He tried to convince his parents and his children that Abby had abandoned them all. Easy and typical for him, because Abby was not available to tell her side of the story.

God Furnishes an Apartment

Searching for an apartment in San Diego, with not so good credit was going to be hard. Even if Abby could find a guardian angel to let her rent a place, how would she be able to furnish it. Her soon to be ex, made sure Abby knew, after five years of marriage, everything in their house was his. Everything. Abby was not entitled to any of it. He laid claim to everything for the sake of their kids. Minute by minute, hour by hour, our family in Arizona was hit with the reality that Abby needed an apartment and some furniture. Abby informed Miranda, that she had a blow-up air mattress, a camping chair, and the clothes Deb and Miranda brought to her in the hospital. Miranda, our little prayer warrior, Abby's big sister, said, "Everyone, just start praying. Pray someone will give Abby a chance. She had a job; a good job. She has reliable transportation. Lord, Abby just needs a place for her and her kids to live."

As her release date drew closer and closer, Abby and Miranda talked often about her housing possibilities. Anytime Abby had the opportunity to talk to an actual apartment manager or rental company, she would tell her story. Each time, she hoped someone, anyone with room in their heart, would have a room for her and her kids. After numerous attempts, Abby came across another earthly angel, a woman who had a two-bedroom apartment, who was willing to give Abby a chance. Abby had been transparent with her potential landlord, her credit was not great, but Abby had three qualities she admired. Abby was honest, a hard worker, and a single mom wanting a better life for herself and her children.

Miranda started painting a picture in her mind, an image of her niece and nephew, finally able to spend time with their mom after being in a group home for two months, but they would not have a bed to sleep on. Her niece and nephew would have no toys. They would have no stuffed animals, no blankets, no pillows, nothing. To Miranda, and to us, it felt like the Grinch had stolen Christmas from Cindy Lou Who all over again. We all had a fairly good idea who would play the part of the Grinch. Miranda's image was spiraling out of control, her thoughts were racing, but more importantly, she was on her knees praying for a big miracle.

Brandon and Miranda are two of the most frugal people we know. They can stretch a dollar to last and last, and they know how to save and how to manage their money. At the time Abby was looking for a place, Miranda and Brandon had already been using their envelope system faithfully. Each time they brought income in, Miranda or Brandon would put a little away in their respective envelopes. One of these envelopes was marked "Mad Money" or another way to say, "Spending Money." When they started their envelope system, Miranda and Brandon agreed, they would use it for whatever they wanted to, as long as they both agreed on the item, one hundred percent. They could spend it on a date night, go to the movies, or keep adding a little more each month until they were ready for a big-ticket purchase. They learned over and over; their envelope system had taught them patience.

Miranda peeked inside the "Mad Money" envelope and found two hundred dollars. One night, Miranda shared her thoughts with Brandon. With $200, Miranda was confident she could get herself to and from California. She went on to tell Brandon her plan. She could fill the back of their van with whatever Miranda could collect. Miranda thought they might even use the money to buy a few more things at Goodwill or some thrift shops. She did not have to plead her case; within minutes, Brandon was in support of her plan. That was not the full plan. Miranda had added to her image a van full of household items and started reaching out to friends. She only had one question, "Do you have any extra household or personal items I could gift to my younger sister, niece, and nephew?"

What she did not know is that God had not fully revealed his plan either. Two of Miranda's friends posted a short summary of Abby's story and Miranda's "Fill the Van Plan" on Facebook. Meanwhile, Miranda was measuring the inside of her van to determine if there would be enough room for a couple of twin sized mattresses. If she removed all the back-passenger seats, Miranda was certain the area would be big enough to hold two mattresses and so much more. Now, with God at the helm, she waited for His plan to play out.

Hours after her friends had made the post of the two sisters, people started messaging her friends saying, "I have a couch; I have a chair; I have toys; I have a bed frame; I have a dresser; I have a mattress." The whole "Fill the Van Plan" started to snowball in an amazing way. By the end of the day, the snowball was rolling downhill, full speed ahead, and had no signs of slowing down. After the post had been live for one day, Miranda's friends reached out to her to let her know what each of the messengers was offering. Our little prayer warrior now had a bigger task ahead. She had to start collecting.

Her next few days were a happy blur of blessings. Miranda would show up to the address she had been messaged and the people would say, "I have a couch; it's kind of worn, but you can have it." Not, "This is how much I want for it," but "You can have it!" Miranda did not know what to expect after each description. As she stepped into the messenger's family room, Miranda smiled when she saw an adorable set of bright red couches, a coffee table, and two matching side tables. The next address had the perfect kitchen table with three chairs. Before she could even ask how much, the messenger stated, "You can have it." All day, as Miranda continued to pick up item after item, and a new image was being revealed. Abby's new apartment was going to be furnished, and the furnishings were genuinely nice pieces. As Miranda's heart grew bigger that day, she realized the Grinch was not going to win. Abby's new home was going to look amazing.

As Miranda was about to pick up the last of the items from more well-meaning messengers, another thought blossomed.

She picked up her phone and texted her sister. Abby, if you could create a wish list, a list of all the things you could envision for your new home, what would be on that list? Miranda finished the text, "Abby, just for fun, send me your list" and hit send. Miranda waited for her to respond. A few minutes later, the familiar ping alerted her a new text had arrived. The first item on Abby's list was a vacuum cleaner. As her dad, I can relate to such an important item having top billing. Miranda thought it was odd and texted her back, "This is a wish list and you want a vacuum cleaner?" Abby continued texting; "Yes, I would love a vacuum cleaner. I would like floor mats for my kitchen, the squishy mats you can stand on when you do the dishes. I would like some lamps and a side table for my camping chair. I wish I had dressers for the kids. And I wish the drawers were all filled with new clothes." As Miranda scrolled through her text, Miranda was mentally checking everything off what had already been gifted. Miranda stopped to thank God for everything He had done to move so many to donate, but secretly Miranda was hoping God had a plan for some of the missing items on the wish list.

The next day, Miranda was telling one of her clients all the things people donated. Caught up in the story, Miranda's client told her she had a couple of things in her garage she was going to give to Goodwill and Miranda was welcome to come look at them. As Miranda stepped into her client's garage, there sat a vacuum cleaner and two matching lamps. The last two items Miranda had yet to check off. As Miranda drove away, she was thinking two things, "God, you are amazing, so unbelievably amazing." Second, "How am I ever going to get all of these gifts to California? They would never fit in my van."

Miranda was about to head to California, and she was so excited to share the results of the "Fill the Van Plan" post to all who would listen. Brandon and Miranda's Dairy Queen buddy, Brian, inquired how her little sister was doing. He already knew she was desperately trying to get back on her feet. Miranda joyfully shared, "Abby is done with rehab. She is starting a new chapter and let me tell you, God is so good." Miranda went on to explain, "Now, I just have to figure out how I will get everything to her." Suddenly, Brian said, "Miranda, hold on a minute." When Brian came back on the phone he said, "Okay, I want to pay for the U-Haul. It clearly sounds like you will need a U-Haul. Can I pay for it?" What could she say? Miranda asked God to provide a way, and he did! Brian provided Miranda his information, and within a few hours, the U-Haul was in her driveway, and she started to fill it up. When she finished, Miranda and Brandon stood back in amazement, it was literally packed to the roof, from top to bottom. Miranda truly had to contain herself when she casually called Abby to say she would be leaving in the morning and she had a few items to go with her air mattress and camping chair.

As Miranda left Arizona with a U-Haul overflowing with fulfilled wishes, she realized she had not spent a single dollar of their "Mad Money." She would wait until she arrived in San Diego to see what Abby and her kids might need. Miranda had never driven a truck of this size before. Her prayer, "God, you got me this far, now get me, and this truck safely to California." She found her favorite praise and worship station on the truck radio and happily drove for six hours until she arrived in downtown San Diego, close to Abby's new apartment. As the unfamiliar streets started to narrow, with numerous cars on either side of the truck, Miranda's fear of scratching a parked car grew. After a few close calls, Miranda was certain if she drove another foot, she would take off a random side mirror of an innocent car. Ever so slowly, rolling forward, she came to a stop sign and dialed Abby's number. Abby yelled into the phone, "You're here! I don't see you. I don't see the van." Miranda smiled and said, "I'm right in front of you." Abby replied, "What are you talking about? I don't see you!"

As Abby looked up and down the street, Miranda sat up taller in her U-Haul, grinning as their eyes met. Abby then realized Miranda was in the big U-Haul sitting at the stop sign, not the van she was expecting. Miranda recalls the jaw-dropping look on Abby's face was priceless. She will never forget how her mouth just fell wide open. Abby hopped up and peered in the window of the driver's side and said, "I don't know where you will park this truck. You will probably need to move it to the back of the apartment." Miranda pushed open the door, stepped down and out of the driver's seat, and happily announced, "I'm not driving this thing an inch further. I am scared to drive it. Your turn."

Abby willingly jumped into the driver seat while Miranda jumped into the passenger's side of the cab and watched Abby maneuver the U-Haul to the back of her apartment. Once safely parked, Abby opened up the rear sliding door of the truck and Miranda could clearly see, Abby was stunned. Abby was having trouble finding words to ask, "How did this happen?" As they started to take small items out of the truck, Miranda repeated the story of how her friends, the hearts of some strangers, and their God furnished Abby's entire apartment. Miranda went on to tell her, it was all donated, including the truck. It was unbelievable. God is amazing.

As they walked toward the apartment building, Abby told Miranda that her apartment was on the third floor. So, for the next few hours, two women, one five-foot-two and the other five-foot-three, unloaded an entire U-Haul carrying couches, mattresses, dressers, lamps, tables, chairs, a vacuum cleaner, and absolutely everything on her wish list, into Abby's two-bedroom apartment. Once everything was in, the two girls started arranging and rearranging all the pieces, creating a charming, colorful, and remarkable new home. The next phase was decorating. Miranda did not forget to bring pieces of fabric to reupholster the chairs. Together, they cleaned and painted walls with warm soothing colors. Miranda finally used some of the two hundred dollars to buy some paint. They did not have cable, but now Abby and her kids would have a TV and a DVD player. Miranda brought one movie with her, *Pitch Perfect*. For three days, they listened to that movie and sang all the songs over and over and over. They laughed; they cried; they shared an experience, and only two sisters, two mothers, knew how important these three days would be for Abby and her children.

Together, the sisters knew God had provided everything Abby and her two children would need. They wanted for nothing, and the next chapter in Abby's story was ready to begin. The final touch in the kids' new bedroom was a comforter for each of the twin-sized beds. A bed for each of them, a dresser of clothes, and a closet filled with more clothes, games, books, and toys. Miranda and Abby thought these comforters were the final item to wrap up everything for the kids, just as God had wrapped his big arms around Miranda's "Fill the Van Plan." When all was complete, with her sister settled into her newly furnished home, Miranda was ready to head back to Phoenix. There was just enough "Mad Money" to buy a one-way plane ticket back to Arizona after Miranda dropped off the U-Haul. Both my girls know without a doubt, God not only showed up that weekend, God showed off.

A Tale of Two Oxen

God had an amazing start for Abby and her two children, Khloe, and Garrett. We would've like to say that moving forward as a divorced single mom, it would've been better. Some months were easier than others, but some were hard. Abby struggled most with the loneliness. At least she thinks it was loneliness, I lean more toward codependency. Codependency made it easier for her to walk the path of addiction. As a married couple, they were not good for each other. Even a divorce, an affair, painful kid pickups and drop offs, only compounded the extreme bouts of sadness. She convinced herself being single was hard. But then again, being together with someone who does not walk the same journey you are taking with your God, is extremely hard. A message from a long-ago sermon reminded me, singleness is not a curse; it is a gift. Paul says it is a gift to be spent wisely and used sensibly. You always have incredible opportunities as a single person but most of the time when you are in that season, all you want is the next one. If you are too impatient, then when it seems like God's plan is taking longer, you try to fast forward His plan. In other words, we want to microwave something that is supposed to be in a crock pot. Here is what the Bible also says, a Christian dating a Non-Christian is like giving two oxen the task of pulling a wagon. You can put a yoke on two oxen, but in order to carry the load, the yoke needs to be evenly distributed. If it is not, one of them will have a heavier weight than the other. What happens then is that one will begin to pull stronger than the other one, and you will slowly start to veer until eventually you just start spinning in circles. All the while, the oxen are under the illusion they are making progress. The truth is, you are just spinning in circles and going nowhere.

Through the years there was extreme pushing and pulling with the stubborn ox whose primary concern was about having his own needs met. This usually meant he would manipulate the people in his life in order to meet those needs. Abby and her ex had a mostly off relationship that was complicated and complex. On the surface, what he wanted people to see was a doting father, an attentive ex-husband, and a supportive co-parent. Below the surface, his addictions were so strong, if anyone got in his way, he would swat them away, like an annoying fly. After being homeless for a year and limited contact with his children, he reappeared in their lives with a whirlwind of empty promises. When his daughter discovered he was sneaking bottles of alcohol into our house, he tried to convince her brother and mother that she was a snitch. He told his son, if he had to limit his visits because of her snitching, it would be his sister's fault.

Our youngest son was frightened after he overheard him taunting and berating the police on the phone when he was trying to avoid them after causing a hit and run while under the influence. Our son was so worried the ex would show up at our house with the same anger, we had to go to court and get an order of protection, so he could feel safer. Somehow, the order of protection was our fault, because Deb and I did not understand the pressures he was under trying to conceal yet another woman he was playing house with.

For too long, we watched similar events play out week after week. Abby's ex never took responsibility for his own actions. We had seen enough. We had grown weary of witnessing his repetitive, self-serving, narcissistic behaviors. To get our point across, I chose to write Abby a series of seven texts. Again, the number seven would prove to be significant.

I told her I had prayed and asked God to send me the words I needed for her to read. As I sat in my car in silence for seven mornings, God blessed me with the words and the phrases I put into these texts. I was always amazed at what my fingers had typed each morning before I hit send. With each day, I felt hope rising inside me. Hoping and praying, "Please, let Abby listen to her heavenly father because she is ignoring her earthly one." Together, God and I called these series of texts the *"7 Day Cleanse."*

THE 7 DAY CLEANSE

DAY ONE: Take the Day Off

So, mom shared that you two had talked and you were pretty sad last night about how things keep playing out and you may not go to work today. You are no longer a sassy teenager; you are an adult, so it is okay if you choose not to go to work. If you do choose not to go today, then take the day off.

But tomorrow you need to get back to business as usual. Abby, you need to be back at work and continue to take care of your family. Try not to get inside your head. Take this day just to process, are you actually getting off the merry-go-round or will you stay on for a longer ride?

Abby, we hope you will get off, and you will stay off. Take the day off from texting him or returning his calls. If you accomplish no other thing today, at least turn off your phone. All texts and phone messages will be there when you turn your phone back on tomorrow. A day off, a day of rest, a reprieve from toxic texts and rants, hearing everything is your fault. Do yourself a huge favor and do not respond for one day. Just one day.

I am going to send you one text every day for a total of seven days. I am not even asking you to read them each day. Just do not delete them yet. After seven days, take a few minutes to read each one, process each day, and then see how you feel. In seven days, I am going to check in with you again and you can tell me then what you are thinking. Mom and I are here to support you and we will continue to do that even if you continue to stay on the merry-go-round for a little while longer. We pray you will eventually get tired of the endless, exhausting, tedious ride. We know this is not the life you want to lead. We pray for you every day and will never stop praying for you.

DAY TWO: Focus on Family. Your Son.

Last night you mentioned you were processing how you would explain to your kids that they would not be seeing their dad this week. Not sure if you will actually go through with this, but if you want my sage advice, be truthful with them. Just let your son know, his dad decided once again to choose himself and some other person over his son. While it does not mean he is a horrible human being, it just means he has free will. The beautiful thing — you and your son have free will as well. Now is the time to show your son the man you want him to be.

How fitting for a great lesson, Valentine's Day. You do not want your son to be confused about how to treat women, especially one he might be interested in or care about someday. You want your son to show women respect. So, you are choosing to not expose him to someone who would continually demonstrate disrespectful behaviors. Yes, your son will be sad. Eventually, you will work out a new visitation plan for him and his dad. Your son needs to trust that you know what is best for him. Focus on the family. Focus on your son. Then, one day when you meet your future daughter in law, she will pull you off to the side and say thank you. Thank you, for raising a son who is so kind, attentive, considerate, and such a gentleman.

DAY THREE: Focus on the Family. Your Daughter.

Getting your son to understand and accept he might not be seeing his dad was not going to be an easy task. But, if you have stayed away from his toxic texts, I am guessing it was doable. If you are still not sure about your path, still riding this merry-go-round, it is important you focus on your daughter today. She will surprise you. She already informed you a few nights ago, she does not want to go backwards. She does not want to be the parent again and have to be the person to take care of her brother. She has years of memories where her parents were both using, and those people were not dependable. She has shared with her grandparents on a few occasions she does not believe her dad is the right person for her mother. If we could choose sides, as we look into your daughter's eyes, we would choose her. She is older, she understands how history repeats itself, and she wants off this emotional merry-go-round, too.

We are not surprised she is confused about what to do if any boy shows interest in her. Why would she let someone hurt her heart like she has seen with her parents over and over? We believe she will remain guarded because she has watched you waver back and forth over a man who brings you to tears again and again. This pattern will continue with each new young man that comes into her life, until she settles for a guy like her dad and experiences hurt after hurt after hurt. She will be emotionally exhausted and one day ask you, "why did you settle?"

Abby, we are praying every morning and every night before our heads hit that pillow you will focus on you and your beautiful children. Please place all your energy, all your finances, all your attention, on your babies. When you fill their weekends with your affection, your children will not feel the loss of their dad's physical presence. Give your son and daughter one of the greatest gifts, a gift that will cost you nothing. Your time. They are already familiar with the antics of the person who has never put them first. Help your daughter witness how a mother's love always puts her child first.

DAY FOUR: Your Mental and Physical Health.

Are you really saying it is over? Could it really be true? What will happen in a few days when he sobers up, calling and texting, asking for forgiveness. He screwed up. He is so sorry. He wants to see the kids. Help a guy out. Woe is me. Then, if you say, "not yet," the mean drunk will come back with a vengeance. He will go into a rant about what a terrible mother you are. Damn, this gets old, doesn't it? Will it change? Can it change? Can you change?

Here is your chance to change a pattern forever. You are at a crossroads today. Your focus should not be on a person who is self-centered, always entitled, always finding fault in you. You need to focus on your own personal mental health.

You have already taken great strides on this journey. Prepping foods on the weekend, eating better, and seeing your counselor each week. We were thankful you followed up on the names of the Christian counselors we shared with you. Even though each session may bring up painful memories, the process, the efforts, and the progress will bring about a healthier you. If you should falter and feel sorry for this man, you might consider seeking out a codependency expert. You are tracking towards a healthier you. You have been talking about losing some weight. I think if you were to rid yourself of a 190 lb. male, that would be the best weight loss solution for all.

Mental wellness flourishes when you are no longer hiding or keeping things bottled up. The truth sets you free. It is time to trust God to give you the courage to cleanse yourself of his burdens and you and your children can truly start healing.

DAY FIVE: Spirituality and Faith

On this journey, you have seen God showing up and showing off on numerous occasions. People seldom lose their faith because of a one-time event. Instead, their faith slowly erodes because they do not use it. Your faith depends on our relationship with God. This connection is a lot like any other relationship we have with people, if we do not pay attention to that person or persons, the relationship can fade away. It does not mean the person still is not present in our life; it just means the relationship languishes from a long lack of attention. So, keeping your faith alive and vibrant takes energy and focus and the discipline of being around those who can stimulate you towards a deeper faith. This is why Mom and I go to church every Saturday or watch Rock Point Live if we are out of town. Just like breakfast, lunch, and supper, you need sustenance to survive. That is what church does for us. It feeds us and keeps our relationship with God strong.

Nothing makes your heart swell more as a parent than sitting next to your adult children in church. Having a conversation on how the lesson or sermon affected them is sweet icing on the cake. As you walk through this next season and your

relationship with Christ, the importance of keeping your relationship fed and feeding your children's faith is so important.
In the near future, your son and your daughter will need to call
on God more and more, especially if their father is still in their
lives. Help yourself, then help them, stay on a faithful journey.

DAY SIX: Finances

I hope you have looked over these texts each day. I hope
they are mulling around inside your thoughts and you can stop
and breathe. Process and ponder. Initially, when a parent talks
about financial responsibilities, it is the time to talk about first
paying your rent, making your car payments, your insurance
payments, keeping food on the table, and utilities. We only
had to have that talk with you a few times. Then you found
your rhythm and we never had to talk to you again until he
came into your life. Then, all our life lessons went out the
window because someone convinced you those lessons were
outdated, stupid, and they did not serve his purpose.

You know, he actually taught us a lesson once. Because of
his behaviors, we learned never to give cash. We have paid for
the electricity directly to the electric company. We have made
car payments directly to the bank. We have learned not to give
cash to anyone who is not honest.

To assist with a twelve-pack of soda or a couple of other
items at the grocery store, with an offer to pay us back, that
is a win-win. Abby, when you have helped him financially and
he has no intention of paying you back, that is simply wrong.
When he takes advantage of your sister and takes their money
and does not finish the work. That is just sad. That is what
you call lose-lose. Please, protect your hard-earned money.
Your ex-husband expects people to take care of him, provide
for him, and then he even resents people when they do not
offer to help. That is wrong. You work hard. You budget your
finances, and you save when you can. You are making strides

and you do not need him to take advantage of you anymore. You need to provide for your family, pay your bills, not his. He needs to be a man and earn his own way.

DAY SEVEN: *Tough Love*

We know that once upon a time, you loved the father of your children and the potential he had. But, you said it best. It has been years, and you keep hoping and hoping he would change, or he might grow up. Here he is, as an adult, and he never stopped blaming other people for his mistakes or his own poor choices.

What has never changed for us, is our love for you. We love you enough to open our doors until he selfishly brought alcohol into our home, then called his own daughter a snitch. We love you enough that we encouraged others to welcome him into their homes and give him work, only to learn that he took advantage of their kindness, too. We love you enough to share our home with your children even though he spoke poorly of us whenever he had the chance. We can see how his stories and his lies exhaust you and bring you to tears. We understand, even half of the truth is still a whole lie. Aren't you tired of the lying?

Finally, we love you enough to know we have seen and heard enough. If you do decide to choose him over your chil-dren, we strongly encourage you to find an exit strategy for yourself. You may allow him back in your heart, your home, your life, but we never will. We love you enough to say: WE ARE DONE. We are done with your narcissistic ex-husband's behaviors. We hope and pray you are too.

—

That was the final text I sent from the "Seven Day Cleanse" experiment. Deb and I could not be certain that seven days would be enough. The number seven had proven to be significant in my life for other reasons. Could these words that God put on my heart, impact Abby in a life-changing way?

After seven days of texts, Abby stepped off the merry-go-round. She may never admit to her parents that the seven-day cleanse was a decisive influencer to not purchase another ticket and get off that tiresome ride. We would like to think that God's messages made an impact. We would like to think God's words became healing words and gave her more strength.

We know that 2020 has been a difficult year for many people. As you finished this chapter, you learned what happened in the last thirty years of Abby's life. I am hoping you are curious about how God has shown up for her again. It was Abby's desire to achieve two big milestones by the time she turned thirty-five. At the beginning of 2020, Abby took the job of her dreams, working for one of the largest pediatric healthcare systems in the country. In the time Abby has been with PCH, she has received numerous commendations and accolades from her supervisors, the doctors, and the patients she works with. They undoubtedly see what we have always known about her caring heart and deep dedication to her job and her children. After living with us for three years, Abby will be receiving the keys to a new home in November. A picture-perfect three-bedroom home for a blessed family of three. What has honestly made her heart full, was the message her daughter gave her after she signed the paperwork to start building their dream home. Khloe wanted to remind her mother how strong and courageous she has been, "Mom, you accomplished everything dad promised, but could not deliver. Everything!" Abby, Khloe, and Garrett are eagerly awaiting to see what God has planned for 2021.

No matter what Abby's future brings, we will continue to commit to this daughter, as well as all of our children, even those who are not biologically ours.

8

LOVE LESSONS

S tephany Kayleen came into our lives when she was only two days old. It was New Year's Eve, 2005, as we took the call from the Department of Child Safety and the Mesa General Hospital looking for a temporary placement. The hospital was hoping for a short-term foster home with some medically fragile experience because this newborn had Down's Syndrome, pulmonary issues, cataracts on both eyes, and was drug-exposed. Even with only three years fostering in Arizona, it was not unusual for us to get a placement call for such an infant; we had already cared for seven drug-exposed babies.

We Are Keeping This One

According to the nurses, DCS had called five other families on this holiday weekend and received a "No" from each one. The nurse also shared with us that Mesa General had a Woman's Care Clinic, offering free pregnancy testing and prenatal care. However, there was no record at Mesa General that this newborn's mom had any prenatal care prior to the delivery three days ago. None of that mattered to us and we accepted the placement.

When Deb arrived at Mesa General, she was escorted by a security guard to a waiting room. The guard motioned with a nod of his head and whispered that the woman standing at the desk was the infant's mother. In the waiting room, a nurse told Deb the infant girl was baby number five for this mom. All her children were still in her care, but after Stephany was born, all five were placed in foster care. The mom had named her Stephany Kayleen. Early post-delivery screenings indicated this baby girl's eyes were both covered with cataracts. Other checks indicated that Stephany had been exposed to cocaine, meth, and marijuana. When the nurses told Stephany's biological mother that she tested positive for drugs and Down's Syndrome, she thought the doctor could just give her baby a shot, and she would be better. Stephany's birth mom had never heard of Down's Syndrome.

The nurses asked Deb if we were still okay to meet baby Stephany, even though she had so many medical issues. Deb agreed, and they walked her to the nursery. Deb told me later that when the nursery placed baby Stephany in her arms, she fell madly in love with Stephany's dense, milky white eyes and rosy apple cheeks. Stephany was seven pounds of substance-exposed sweetness. When Deb arrived home from the hospital, she placed a car seat on the kitchen table announcing, "We're keeping this one!" Flustered, I said, "Wait a minute! Remember, we are a bridge; we care for them until their biological parents are able to do it themselves." I was pretty sure I talking to myself.

A baby like Stephany was new for us; a baby with Down's Syndrome. We did not have any experience with this genetic disorder, but Deb had already brought Stephany home. We missed the festive ball drop in Times Square as we researched everything we could possibly find about potential medical issues. Children with Downs's Syndrome typically have several health problems: low muscle tone, sleep apnea, thyroid issues, congenital heart defects, and chronic pulmonary disorder.

Some children with these disorders may also have intellectual disabilities. Based on what we read, Deb and I feared more and more; Stephany's biological mother had exposed her unborn daughter to drugs and alcohol throughout her entire pregnancy. By daylight, we were convinced Stephany would need parents who could fully commit for this baby to survive.

Once you take in any foster child, especially a newborn, within 24 to 48 hours you must bring the infant to a recommended pediatrician. Deb made an appointment at Phoenix's Children's Hospital in Phoenix. Stephany's checkup would not be with the regular pediatrician Deb had brought some of our other substance-exposed babies to. This new doctor assigned to us appeared to be extremely nervous, especially about her eyes. After a few minutes, he stopped the examination and just left the room. The first doctor came back with someone else. This new doctor looked at her eyes and announced this four-day-old had severe cataracts. The second doctor informed Deb that infantile cataracts were not uncommon with alcohol or illicit drug use during pregnancy.

Stephany's cataracts were so dense, they masked the true color of her eyes. Before Deb left her first appointment, Stephany had another one with the top Pediatric Ophthalmologist at Phoenix Children's. At the appointment, her pediatric specialist thought we should do Stephany's surgery right away. Hindsight is perfect. Perhaps, we should have waited more than three weeks; perhaps, we should have waited until Stephany was stronger. Had we waited longer; Stephani's lungs may have been more fully developed. Had we waited longer; Stephany may not have contracted pneumonia. Had we waited; we may not have been excluded from the first year of Stephany's life.

Some children with Down's Syndrome are susceptible to chronic pulmonary issues. What we learned with Stephany; she was more susceptible to infections after a surgery with anesthesia. In her case, the symptoms would manifest a few days later, with retracted breathing, a chronic cough, and a fever. A follow-up visit with our pediatrician resulted in a pre-scription of Ibuterol for Stephany. A quick-relief medication, Ibuterol, is often used to prevent and treat wheezing or short-ness of breath caused by an assortment of breathing problems. After we picked up her prescription, I was setting up Stephany's breathing machine when the phone rang. Deb recognized the number of our case manager, so I told her to take that call and I would start Stephany's breathing treatment. I was only into the treatment a few minutes when Stephany went limp and her face took on a gray tint, then blue. I stopped the treatment and told Deb to hang up. We must go to the hospital, now.

We lived very close to the Chandler Hospital and their Emergency Room. We were in the car and driving towards the hospital in a few precious seconds. As I carried Stephany through the doors, I could see her face had gained a pinkish hue, but her breathing was very labored. The nurses took one look at our fear-stricken faces our baby's limp body and rushed us into a curtained room. The staff attached a pulse oximeter. This electronic device quickly measures the satura-tion of oxygen carried in your red blood cells. Normally one should have an oxygen saturation somewhere between 80 and 100 percent. Stephany's first oxygen reading was at 60, and the crisis team immediately put a nasal cannula to deliver supple-mental oxygen and increase Stephany's airflow. Within min-utes her levels were reading in the '70s, then the '80s. Once Stephany was stabilized, we were able to tell the team about the Ibuterol breathing treatment I had tried to give her; the Emergency Room connected the dots and strongly suggested Stephany may be deathly allergic to this medication.

If, for any reason, you make an emergency room visit with a foster child, the incident must be reported to your case man-ager. As Deb was on the phone with Stephany's case man-ager, I could hear Deb's frustrated inquiry, "If the state had placed this child in our care to begin with, why would they question her safety now?" The conversation appeared to be very one-sided. Deb would try to provide the case manager with more information, but the case manager on the other end of the phone was firm. DCS would gather more information, but Stephany would remain in the hospital's care until a decision was made. Deb was hurt and frustrated by everyone who questioned her in the next few days. She told every person involved with Stephany's case that, when she was released, she could devote her full attention to Stephany, because we did not have any other foster kids. In fact, she offered to sit by her bedside 24 hours a day if needed. Her suggestions, statements, and demands fell on non-listening ears. Two days into Stephany's hospital stay, Deb and I were notified that a new foster family had been assigned to her case, and Stephany would not be going home with us.

Deb was introduced to Stephany's new foster mom, who immediately told Deb she already had a couple of foster kids at home and could not possibly be at the hospital all the time. Deb was furious. This is what the state thought was best for this baby? To be left alone in a hospital until her new mommy could find time to be with her?! On January 30, a month later, Deb signed the papers to release Stephany to her new foster family. She sat down in the rocking chair, held her as close as she could and, whispered in Stephany's ear, "I love you, baby girl, I will find a way so we can be together!" Deb said her final goodbyes and left the room in tears. Deb was sitting in her car, the tears flowing freely, when her phone rang. Deb recognized Miranda's number. Thinking Miranda was probably curious how the transfer went, Deb answered her call. Much to her surprise, "Mom, I'm in labor, can you please come to the hospital?" Deb told me later, "I looked to the heavens, 'Fine God, I get it. I'm needed elsewhere.' Kyan Jay Andree was born on January 31st. Kyan had mild jaundice, so he would require light therapy and a special blanket of fiber-optic lights upon his release from the hospital. Even though these items are designed to help, Brandon and Miranda were nervous. However, if they followed the regiment established by the hospital, Kyan's jaundice could clear up in a couple of weeks.

Four days later, Deb received a devasting call from her Mom and Dad. Deb's niece had been killed in a car accident. With Kyan safely in a doctor's care, our foster beds empty, Deb decided she was needed back in Stewartville. Six months earlier, her parents had buried another son, Dale. He had suffered a fatal heart attack at 57-years-old. Now, his 33-year-old daughter was gone, too. There were times in the early years of our marriage where we were not certain how much pain and heartache both our parents could withstand. My parents — Fred and Marilyn — had buried two children, both who left behind spouses with newborns. Now, Deb's parents — Ken and Maxine — had buried two sons and soon a beloved granddaughter. Deb stayed in Minnesota for the next three weeks offering comfort to her family, but Stephany was never far from her mind. Deb was formulating a plan that would help both Stephany's new foster mom, as well as allow Deb to be close to the sweet baby girl she desperately wanted to call our daughter.

Deb knew that Stephany's new foster mom was busy fostering other children as well. Deb also knew, as a busy foster mom herself, you can always use a helping hand. Deb called Stephany's new foster mom and asked if she could come during the afternoons or evenings to just rock Stephany while this mom made meals or whatever she had to do in her bustling busy home. Deb learned that Stephany would be released from the hospital about the time that she would be returning from Minnesota. Knowing that Stephany would need around the clock care, her new foster mommy welcomed the thought of a helping hand. Meanwhile, Deb and I signed up for the classes we needed to complete to receive our Division of Developmental Disabilities license in order to have Stephany come back home to us. Deb had been talking with the Office of Licensing, Certification, and Regulation (OLCR) of Arizona. The OLCR is responsible for issuing Home and Community Based Services certificates. All individuals and provider agencies are required to have an HCBS certificate in order to provide services to DDD members. HCBS Certification ensures that all individuals providing direct care have met all the qualifications for assisting individuals with developmental disabilities. In order to provide care in our home for Stephany, Deb and I needed a list of required classes in attendant care, treatment and training, habilitation, personal care, respite care, therapy services, transportation, and other services designed for DDD members. If we did not miss one session and completed all training required, the Sielings would have their required DDD license in a year.

Deb and Stephany's new foster Mom, Robyn, soon became allies. Deb would make sure every week that she was in contact with Robyn, always accepting any opportunity to cuddle, sing, or to love on Stephany. After a few months of continued bonding, Robyn and her husband, Bill, needed to leave town for a family event. They asked Deb if we could watch Stephany while they were out of town. I am not sure Robyn finished her request before Deb responded in the affirmative, "Yes, we would love to watch Stephany!" We told Robyn and Bill that whenever they needed us, we would be available. This would not be the only weekend we cared for this sweet baby girl. The year of our DDD classes was almost over when we learned the courts were moving to sever Stephany from her biological mom. Typically, after severance, the current foster parents are first asked if they are interested in adoption. Robyn and Bill, knowing the Sielings anxiously hoped to adopt Stephany, informed her caseworker that adoption was not their goal. In the same breath, Robyn and Bill informed the caseworker they knew of a devoted couple that genuinely wanted to adopt her. Robyn proceeded to tell Stephany's caseworker a two year-long story of one woman's determination.

Poor Baby

The reality of Stephany's medical needs came with her the day our sweet but fragile girl moved in. Numerous notes from her frequent doctor visits may give a better perspective of her story:

Stephany is a 14-month old with a history of Down's Syndrome, pneumonia, and intermittent oxygen requirement. Recently, she has had problems with noisy breathing and raspy coughing. She continues Pulmicort twice a day, and Reglan therapy three times a day to help with reflux. She has intermittent nasal congestion and uses a humidifier daily. Her nasal mucosa remains congested and boggy.

At 17months, Flonase has been added daily for maintenance therapy. She did become acutely ill with an upper and lower respiratory tract infection toward the end of March. She does have some noisy upper airway breathing present.

At 21 months, Stephany has continued with Pulmicort for maintenance therapy and using Flonase on a regular basis. She has not required oxygen but was recently started on amoxicillin for problems related to her otitis media, chronic ear infections.

At 24 months, one year, four visits to the emergency room, and thirty-eight doctor appointments later, her doctor's notes read, *Stephany has not required any dosing of bronchodilator therapy. In addition, she had not required any recent use of oxygen. She seems to be handling upper and lower respiratory tract infections quite well, without the need for systemic steroids. No recent fevers. No wheezes or crackles. No retractions. No nasal congestion or evidence of otitis.*

Stephany was severed in August of 2007, two years and eight months after Deb set her on our kitchen table and said, "We are keeping this one!" On October 27, 2007, members of our family drove into the parking lot of the Maricopa County Superior Court building on Javelina Avenue in Mesa for our sweet girl's adoption. Strangely, the parking lot looked abandoned, so we checked the time of the appointment in the letter and then the location. When no other cars arrived in the next few minutes, I went to the door and pressed the call button. A guard came to the door, stuck his head out, and asked if he could help. I told the guard we were here for our daughter's adoption. He informed us, that adoptions were at the Durango Courthouse and this building was closed for the day. He verbally gave us the address to the Durango site. The Superior Court of Arizona on Durango Street in Phoenix was 22 miles away. We had been told by our adoption attorney if we were not there when they called our names, we would have to reschedule. Our two-year journey was evaporating before our eyes.

I distinctly remember; I was worried, I was frustrated, I was speculating aloud wildly. My doubts were winning. Were we even supposed to be doing this? We knew we had our bio-logical children's support, yet Deb's parents had subtly shared their reservations with all of Stephany's medical issues. Could this be the final sign this adoption was not meant to be? Deb kept assuring me, throughout the longest drive in history, everything will be just fine. As we pulled up in front of the courthouse, no one needed to tell me we had one minute to spare. I released a big sigh and sprinted toward the court-house with Stephany in my arms. We were stopped by secu-rity guards and metal detectors. Once we located the judge's chambers at the information desk, I bounded the flight of stairs to the long row of courtrooms. The hallway was empty.

No groups of anxious, excited families waiting. We arrived at our assigned room and pointed to our last name on the docket. Clearly, we all could see that our scheduled time had come and gone. I told myself we had come too far, I exhaled and stepped inside the big door with Stephany still in my arms. I could hear Deb tell me, "Kevin, you can't go in there!" as I was met by a clerk who said that the judge had finished for the day.

Stephany's story came pouring out, her illnesses, her recoveries, her appointments, the incorrect address, the journey we have been on. The clerk raised his hand signaling me to stop; he asked me to wait and stepped inside. Unexpectedly, he came back out, opened the big doors, and ushered all of us into the judge's chambers. Five minutes later, our adoption declaration read Stephany Joy Sieling.

Stephany's early years were occupied with numerous surgeries, constant challenges, and some bittersweet disappointments. During this journey, she has provided us with life lessons that have filled our hearts with tolerance, tenderness, and joy. Stephany's first life lesson came in the form of patience. As experienced parents, we were familiar with the expected milestones for newborns and toddlers, but sadly we saw them come and go for Stephany. Even though children with Down's Syndrome can be extremely limber and flexible, Stephany never learned to crawl. Stephany would roll on the hard floor from room to room to get where she wanted to go. Then, at age three, she sat up and started scooting across the tile floors on her butt. Eventually, we tried a walker and a bouncer to strengthen her legs and prayed someday Stephany would walk.

Our biological family continued to grow and flourish. As our Evan and his fiancé made their wedding plans, he thoughtfully requested that his little sister be a flower girl. They considerately suggested that we pull Stephany down the aisle in a wagon. We hesitantly agreed to the idea, not knowing Stephany and God had other plans. A few days before their wedding, Stephany took her first steps. We did not tell our son; instead, we surprised him at the airport when I took her out of her stroller and tearfully watched Stephany gingerly take a few steps into her big brother's arms. On his wedding day, Stephany teetered down the aisle on her own; she was five.

We held out little hope that Stephany might speak one day. Because she was nonverbal, we tried to communicate with simple sign language. Even without her speech, Stephany taught us life lessons in determination. Deb would repeat the same hand gestures over and over hoping Stephany would somehow imitate them. Some universal signs like: "more," "dada," "baby" and "candy;" seemed to stick. Other attempts resulted in random jerky movements, and we made our best guess at what Stephany was trying to tell us. As parents, you must remain steadfast and have a strong faith in prayer when your child cannot speak or communicate simple human needs like: "I'm hungry," "I'm thirsty," or "I hurt."

Miraculously, God has given Stephany the ability to say two words very clearly, "All Done!" It is more of a whisper and it comes out in one breath, "alldone." With a limited vocabulary, Stephany is still able to communicate unmistakably when she is all done eating, all done playing on her iPad, all done riding in the car to her numerous doctor appointments, all done with an exhaustive day, or when she just wants to sleep. Each evening, with great resolve, Stephany whispers "alldone" as she does a little jig on her way to bed.

When Stephany first started school, some of her new teachers were expecting one thing but got another. For those that thought Stephany would be a sweet child who could fit perfectly into their special needs' programs, they quickly found out she did not fit seamlessly. Amid feelings of fear and anxiety, Stephany taught us life lessons in resilience. At school, there were times when Stephany would try to participate without incidence, and then there were anxious days when she would try to hurt herself. The number of drugs that Stephany had been exposed to in utero damaged the portion of her frontal lobe that moderates self-injurious actions.

These unsafe behaviors started without any warning signs. On a crisp January morning, Stephany and I were walking to our car after Sunday school. I was holding her hand, balancing my bible and her therapy ball with my free hand; her diaper bag hanging on my shoulder. With no precursory indicators,

Stephany dropped to the ground and sat down. The next thing I saw was Stephany slamming her head on the hard pavement. Before I could stop her, she had smashed her forehead three times. Her growing bump was deep purple, and blood was running down her face. I snapped Stephany up in my arms, left my scattered belongings in the parking lot, and frantically carried her to our car. I grabbed an article of clothing and held it on her head. When Deb arrived with the other kids, Stephany was sobbing and so was I.

In the days, weeks, and months ahead, we rarely left her alone. If Stephany was not trying to slam her head on a wall, the toilet, the floor, or the back of a chair — she was hitting herself in the face. To soften the force of each blow, we concocted layers of padding, using towels and blankets to cover the dining room table, kitchen chairs, the edge of the bathtub, the toilet tank, even car doors, and windows. Wherever we moved through the house, Deb or I would hold her hands tightly to prevent her from dropping to the tile floors. Several restless months later, Stephany's doctors were able to find the right combination of medications to diminish her self-injurious behaviors. Deb and I look back on how inventive, resourceful, and resilient we had become trying to prevent Stephany from hurting herself.

She Deserves a Chance

Of all her life lessons, Stephany's ability to trust has taught us the most. To trust her teachers to keep her safe during the day when we could not be with her. To trust her doctors to provide her the best care when we no longer had answers. To always trust in God firmly.

When Deb and I thought her self-injurious behaviors were under control, we decided to take a little breather; a vacation. Stephany started hitting herself soon after we left town. When we returned, Stephany had stopped smacking her bruised face.

Then, we noticed Stephany was bumping into furniture, frequently holding an arm out in front of her or cautiously running her fingers along the walls. Stephany would not leave her bed or use utensils to eat. Deb and I were extremely worried. We found ourselves sitting in the consulting room of a new doctor; a retinal eye specialist.

As soon as the doctor entered, he turned off the overhead lighting, leaving the room dark, except for a soft glow from under the cabinets. He pulled out a small pen flashlight from his white coat and slowly moved the beam of light toward our daughter's eyes. First, he started with her right and then switched to her left. As he moved the beam back and forth across her face, I could see her brown eyes gazing forward; there was no change in her dark motionless pupils. Our daughter was showing no reaction to the light. Lord, this could not be true, our sweet Stephany was blind!

After his examination, he caringly explained to us that both Stephany's retinas had detached. The doctor believed the self-inflicted blows to the forehead may have caused some of the damage. He thought, because Stephany's unable to communicate, she may have hit her face thinking she could get her sight back. Nevertheless, without reconstructive surgery, Stephany would be blind. I looked into his sober face and I said, "She has been through so much. We cannot have her endure one more thing. You think there's so much damage; the surgery may not work." He looked at me with great compassion and said, "Doesn't Stephany deserve a chance?"

We were seeking answered prayers and now God was plainly showing us. Trust this doctor. Put Stephany first, relinquish all your doubts, your worries, your fears. Let God guide this surgeon's hands and give Stephany a chance. Without further hesitation, we agreed. Since that first somber day we confirmed Stephany was blind, she has had three surgeries to reattach her retinas and remove scar tissue. The damage to her left eye was beyond repair, but Stephany regained sight in her right eye. With each surgery, Stephany continuously demonstrated unconditional trust.

Love Lessons

When Stephany first went blind, she counted on us to lead her through life. Even now, Stephany still reaches her hand out to us and hangs on tight before she takes any steps. For this moment, we are confident Stephany can see because she will stop in a doorway or in any room of the house, reach back, and flip off the light switch before she leaves a room. Typical of our little teacher, a quick life lesson in frugality. We do not know how long Stephany will have her sight. We are uncertain, but optimistic about her future. We simply have faith that there are more love lessons to come and to share with us, and her future siblings.

9

FINDING HIS VOICE

I n 2000, I was the director of a private school within walking distance of lovely Lake Calhoun in Minneapolis, Minnesota. The small Prekindergarten through Grade 8 school was located on the same site as St. Mary's Greek Orthodox Church. Just as I was finding my rhythm as the new head of school, the parent company out of Colton, California, made the difficult decision to close the school. On the same call, the president of the company offered me an opportunity as the director of a charter school in Chandler, Arizona.

A New Chapter

Deb and I were commuting to Minnetonka, Minnesota every day. First, I would drop Deb off at First Minnesota Bank, and then drive on to the school on Irving Avenue. At home, Evan was a junior at the local high school, and Abby was a sophomore. When the president offered me the position in Chandler, I was thinking, "Evan is going to be a senior, and Abby will be a junior; they will never agree to a move." I could not imagine Evan leaving his high school in his senior year. I thanked my boss for the chance and told him that I would call him back in the morning after talking to my family.

Later at home, I informed Deb and the kids about the offer and how I would be turning it down. Evan, shook his head and held up his hand in a stop position, "Dad, does Chandler, Arizona have a baseball team? If they do, I bet I could play baseball in Arizona every day." I turned my head and looked at Abby. She exclaimed, "I am done with the cold and snow. I bet they do not have snow in Chandler, Arizona. How big is the high school anyway? I am ready for anything bigger right now, count me in." "Okay," I said as I realized I was not even close to predicting their responses. "I'll call my boss in the morning and accept the job. I guess we are moving to Arizona!"

Playing baseball year-round for Evan, and a larger, more diverse peer group for Abby were on their wish lists. Deb and I had not thought about a house with a pool until we flew to Arizona and started house shopping. After spending two days in the valley of the sun, surrounded by rolling hills, mountains, cactus, palm trees, vistas, and exceptional hiking, the Sielings were more than ready to leave the blustery blizzards of Minnesota. We were all ready for a new start in the desert with a backyard pool.

After starting my new director job with the charter school in Chandler, I was really missing Deb and the kids. I had arrived in Arizona during a typical August heatwave, while Deb stayed behind to sell our house. My favorite memory of leaving Minnesota was the morning I placed all my snow shovels and roof rakes on my lawn with a handwritten sign, "Free, Moving to Arizona." Now, my pleasant recollection was overshadowed by the reality of running a school with three times as many students and twice as many staff. This burden was weighing heavy on my heart and my best friend, with who I shared everything, was sixteen hundred miles away. This school had seen three directors in three years, and the faculty was yearning for guidance and clear-cut directions. Waiting for Deb to answer the house phone, I sat down on the bed in my lonely, rented room, staring at the local news where the temperature outside read 105 degrees at 10 pm. As soon as I heard her voice, my eyes misted over. I managed to choke out to Deb, "What was I thinking. I can't do this without you." Deb told me to take a deep breath and then eagerly reported, "We sold the house, and we will be there soon." That message was the one I needed to hear, so I could carry on. With this idea firmly planted, I was ready to refocus my energy in the days and months ahead to promote the school, enroll more families, hire essential staff, and enhance the preschool and grade school programs.

The Sielings flourished in Arizona and I quickly found myself in my third year at the charter school. When you have a school of less than two hundred little bodies, you pride yourself on knowing every student by name and educating yourself on your teaching staff and their families. I had recently hired a new Kindergarten teacher who loved to keep me posted about the high jinks of her small, but lively class. I was not sure who tattled on each other more, her students or her.

The Call to Foster

Every day, she would swing by my office and complain about one of her mischievous students to the most amazing and patient administrative assistant I have ever had, Annette. Mostly she would spout on and on to Annette about all the boys in her class. One day, when Annette had finally heard enough, she quietly tapped on my door to tell me that today's grievance was Michael. I had already heard the story from my open door and knew this teacher was visibly upset that Michael was ignoring her and not sitting down after she ordered him to do so. I acknowledged that I heard her concern, told her to leave Michael with me, and encouraged her to return to class. As she was leaving, I promised to bring Michael back to the classroom after he and I had a chance to chat.

I was a little surprised when I invited Michael to sit down and he could not make eye contact with me. Michael was barely audible, but it was clear, he wanted to stand. As I quizzed Michael about his halfhearted disobedience, his inability to meet my gaze increased my level of concern. I watched him very closely. Next, I mentioned to Michael, I thought it would be best if we would share his refusal with his parents; first, his mom, no response. When I said, "And, your dad, too." Michael winced. The look of fear in his eyes made my stomach flip. I had seen this look before. It felt as if I was holding up a mirror.

An empathetic realization enveloped me. I adjusted my demeanor and started to speak in the most nurturing, comforting voice I could muster. I carefully made my request, "Michael, will you turn around and face that chair?" As he turned ever so slowly, I remember saying, "Thank you. Is it okay if I lift your shirt to see if everything is okay?" Michael began to sniffle, a big tear rolled down his cheek as he nodded in compliance. I gradually raised the hem of his t-shirt. I immediately recognized the crimson colors of fresh bruising on his lower back. I lowered his shirt and told him, "Michael, I am okay if you want to keep standing. You don't have to sit down." As tenderly as I could, I added, "I am going to step outside of my office. I will be right back. Meanwhile, my assistant, Miss Annette, will come inside and sit by you until I return." After confirming the number for Child Protective Services of Arizona, I placed the call and reported what I had discovered.

In a few minutes, the police arrived, and they were in my office talking to Michael. When the officers told Michael he would have to go with them for a ride in their police car, Michael began to openly sob. He looked so frightened. I knew he was in so much physical pain as well. I asked the officers if I could ride along with Michael. They looked at each other and agreed it might be a good idea. I called Deb and told her there had been an incident at school so, I would be home late.

For the next three hours, I sat very close to Michael, sometimes holding his hand, mostly soothing him. I stayed by Michael as he described in his own Kindergarten words how his Daddy hurt him with a big stick. His daddy was mad cause he was late for work. When a woman asked him to change into a gown, I stepped off to the side but kept eye contact with Michael as she helped him strip to his underwear. As Michael stood there, I could see through the open gown the deep red marks all down the backs of his legs. Finally, the man with the camera stopped taking pictures long enough to gesture to the woman. She gently turned Michael to face the wall as she slipped down his underwear. I covered my mouth so Michael could not hear me. Both of his buttocks were a mass of bruises and swelling tissue. With the photographer finished, another woman presented Michael with some new clothes and placed the last piece of Michael's old clothes in a plastic bag.

After another hour passed, another woman arrived, explaining to Michael, as best she could, he was not going home. He would be going to a temporary home, a foster home. I rode with Michael in the back seat of the police car to the home of a frail-looking elderly woman who greeted us all the door. I stood by quietly, holding Michael's hand as the two women exchanged words in whispered breaths. When the paperwork was signed, the officer announced we were leaving. Michael grabbed my shirt sleeve so tight, the officer had to peel his fingers back to release his grip. As soon as I was free, I was ushered out the door. I barely spoke to the officer who gave me a ride back to my school and my car. Before he drove away, I asked if there was any way Michael could have come home with me instead of that foster couple. The officer explained it was possible if I was a licensed emergency home with CPS.

I told Deb the unabridged devastating story when I finally got home, some six hours later. I declared my desire as clearly as I could; I never wanted to leave one of my students in a situation like that ever, ever again. I asked Deb to investigate how we could become an emergency home. Her research resulted in our completing a year-long process to become licensed foster parents.

We fostered for fifteen years, and surprisingly, even after forty-plus foster placements came through our door, only a few pulled so intensely at our hearts. The thought of going through life without two of them would be devastating. First, Stefy, you just read her story. The second little soul that came into our lives, was Edward.

Edward's journey did not begin the same as Stefy's. Deb did not get a call and then go pick him up at the hospital. Strangely enough, Edward was living right next door to us in Chandler, Arizona. In 2009, Deb's first cousin, Sherlyn, and her husband bought the house right next to us. This couple was a part of the Arizona Foster Care system, just like us.

Sherlyn will always be Edward's second mom. If you ever ask Edward about his birth mom, he does not share vivid memories of her, but he always speaks fondly of Sherlyn.

Sherlyn's original placement call for Edward came with a big request from CPS to keep Edward and his siblings all together. CPS had removed Edward along with his two sisters, all very young. Sherlyn knew her limits and offered to take the youngest of the three, the little boy.

When Sherlyn arrived at the CPS office, she found one of the social workers feeding Edward a bottle. Visually Sherlyn could confirm two things. Edward was about eleven months old, and she could sense it had been a long time since he had a bath. The social worker told Sherilyn the staff had gone through an entire container of wet wipes, but they all agreed he desperately needed a bath. Sherlyn also noticed a large knob on the left side of his forehead. The coloring of the bump made her skeptical, even though the social worker indicated his birth mother told them it was a birthmark. Just like Deb,

Sherlyn's first trip with a new placement was straight to her pediatrician. Her doctor confirmed no foul play, it truly was a birthmark. The doctor's office gave Sherlyn a couple of diapers to hold her over after she announced Edward only came into care with two things, a large knob on his head and the one damp diaper he was wearing.

At home, it was time to tackle the smell that permeated around Edward. After running a bath, Sherlyn tried to set him down in the tub, but Edward went a little crazy. Although tiny in size, once he started wiggling, Edward was like a slippery, wet seal thrashing about. Add in a high-pitched wail and bath time was a disaster. Thinking back on Edward's frantic and frightened behaviors, Sherlyn was not certain Edward had ever been in a bathtub. Sherlyn was exhausted by their struggle. Even though Edward was a wee bit cleaner; he was exhausted, too. After toweling him off, Sherlyn wrapped him tightly in a blanket and handed him over to her husband, Mike. After a few seconds of rocking in Mike's arm, Edward was fast asleep and his first day of Foster Care with Mike and Sherlyn was in the books.

Case managers can only share what they are allowed. What Sherlyn and Mike uncovered in the little paperwork they received was an ongoing story of severe negligence and abandonment. Edward's birth father was no longer in the picture, he had been deported back to Guatemala. According to the sporadic and varied police reports, Edward's mom found nothing wrong leaving three toddlers alone while she visited local bars and notorious hangouts.

Mike and Sherlyn did everything they knew as experienced foster parents to help Edward adjust to his new surroundings. What Sherlyn and Deb did routinely for their biological children was positively terrifying for Edward. Whether it was doctor's visits, vaccinations, food shopping, food preparation, baths, or talking to the neighbors — each of these freaked Edward out.

One routine comforted Edward. Sherlyn found that the mat on the bottom of the portable playpen provided Edward with a sense of security. Edward discovered that he could lift the mat and crawl under it. On various occasions, Sherlyn would come into the room to check on Edward, and there he would be, underneath the mat laying on top of the four metal bars that held the playpen in place. Somehow Edward found this particular place and position comfortable, and he would fall fast asleep with the mat on top of him, most likely protecting him from the outside world.

During Edward's year with Sherlyn and Mike, next-door neighbor Deb, would travel back and forth across the yards, facilitating foster placement playdates. When Edward arrived next door, we were fostering the sweetest chubby cherub, I had nicknamed Gus-Gus. I rarely called our placements by the names gifted by their biological parents. After observing and playing with them for a few days, I would announce their new-found names to the family, Hopi-Javi, Shrek, Fiona, J. Lo, Air Jordan, Hailey-Kailey, or Elvis.

Won't You Be My Neighbor?

Edward and Sherlyn became regular visitors to our house. One morning, Sherlyn was getting ready to leave her house. Edward had followed her down the hall and was standing behind the door. Sherlyn reminded Edward they were leaving and grabbed Edward's hand to come with her. As they were leaving the room, Edward reached back with his other hand and stuck it between the frame and door. As Sherlyn recalls, as she was shutting the door behind her, "Just like that, it snapped off the tip of Edward's finger." Edward's familiar scream pierced the stillness; as Sherlyn wrapped his bloody hand in a towel, she picked up Edward in her arms and sprinted next door to tell Deb.

Deb remembers Sherlyn arriving a little hysterical, shouting, "What should I do? What should I do? His finger is gone!" Deb tried to calmly ask, "Where is his finger?" Sherlyn went a little pale and said, "Oh, I don't know. Oh, no, what if Pinto ate it?" Deb rewrapped Edward's injured finger while Sherlyn called 911 and went back to her house to search for the finger. Luckily, the family pet had not gobbled up Ed's finger. They placed his finger in a bag on ice and waited for the ambulance to arrive. At the emergency room, the attending doctor determined they could not reattach the tip of his finger. To this day, Edward's ring finger on his right hand is the same length as his little pinkie.

This incident did not alleviate the symptoms of Edward's attachment disorder. His injury appeared to make his insecurities heighten. Around the same time, Mike and Sherlyn had purchased a new home in Maricopa in Pinal County. After the purchases, they learned that Edward could not leave Maricopa County. How on earth could a child with attachment disorder, who was abandoned by his birth mother, survive moving to another foster home where he wouldn't know anyone? We had come to care deeply for Edward because he was a regular guest at our home. It was not a stretch for us to let Mike and Sherlyn know that we had an open bed, and would be willing to have his case manager place Edward with us. We were all in agreement this would be best for Ed.

Ed slipped into our family routine easily and did so with little anxiety. His apprehensions about the unknown were often visible but multiplied exponentially over inclement weather. Luckily, the weather in Arizona is mostly sunny and warm. However, during the Monsoon season, the weather can change rather quickly. The most spectacular of these weather events are the "Haboobs" or giant walls of dust created from high winds. We could be enjoying a fun afternoon in the pool when the cluster of fronds at the top of our Queen Anne Palm trees would start to sway. As soon as Ed heard this sound, his eyes would widen; he would start to cry and flee inside the house. We were always curious why rough weather was so terrifying for Ed and not so much for other children his age.

Deb and I were required by the state to keep our foster care licensure current by attending classes on relevant topics, such as "Childhood Medical and Behavioral Consequences of Prenatal Cocaine Use." When the case manager transferred Ed's placement to us, we became painfully aware of his birth mother's in-utero substance exposure. With this session, we learned prenatal cocaine and other substance exposure can result in numerous toddler behavior problems. Some clinical reports of toddlers suggested that cocaine-exposed children exhibit patterns of behavioral problems, like elevated fears, aggression, extreme anxiety, poor motivation to learn, difficulty organizing responses, and sudden mood swings. Our biggest epiphany of the day: these sweet children can suffer from an extreme and irrational fear of weather, such as thunder and lightning, known as Astraphobia. By the end of the session, we knew the presenter had fully and accurately described most of Ed's current and possibly future behaviors.

Even with this new insight, as well as the realization that Ed's anxiety would not simply go away overnight, Deb and I were falling in love with this little guy. One evening I looked across the table at Deb and posed the question, "Have you ever thought about adopting Ed?" Deb replied easily with a big smile, "You too?!" Historically, a caseworker will ask near the termination of the biological parents, "If given the opportunity, do you want to adopt this child?" All through our different foster placements, even with those that were with us for two years, Eddie and Stefy were the two that we had both agreed to adopt without hesitation.

Ed's preschool and primary school years were a mixture of highs and lows. Most of his teachers commented on how sweet and handsome he was. Ed did his best to maintain his composure during the school day. However, his mornings and his evenings were not so calm. With Kindergarten and First Grade, his teachers fixated on his inability to focus or stop talking. With second and third grade came timed tests or other opportunities to openly vie against his peers. All of the sudden, time limits or unexpected changes stirred a dormant creature inside him that came out as insecure, frustrating shrieks. As he finished third grade, Ed became very conscious of his peers earning 100% on spelling tests, finishing timed math tests, or completing daily work before he did. What we might consider ordinary occurrences in our elementary years, causes extreme anxiety in Ed's world.

After visits with a psychiatrist and being prescribed much-needed medication, Ed had a bit of calm brought to his world at school. By the end of the day, as the medication wore off, was a completely different story. Homework of any kind and failed efforts to carry out teacher assigned projects were excruciating. Any attempt to correct Ed or offer a different solution, other than his understanding of his teacher's directions, resulted in him screaming back at us, "That's not how my teacher explained it!" I will not even begin to count the number of eraser heads or minutes applied to wipe away what Ed started, and then restarted, in order to meet his altered perception of perfection. Children of substance exposure suffer in silence every day. Imagine a brain that cannot possibly focus, especially when repeatedly asked to pay attention, sit still, or control their behavior around their peers. His days were exhausting.

By fourth grade, his anxiety was so high, his teacher told us that he would hide under his desk, curled up in a tight ball, overwhelmed with tears. This teacher truly understood his struggles; she helped us write a 504 plan for Ed. A 504 plan protects children with any physical or emotional disability which interferes with their capacity to learn in a general education classroom. Ed's 504 plan provided accommodations for his disabilities and was designed to better meet his individual needs and teacher expectations.

Ed struggles with many issues, but the most noticeable are sudden transitions. Abrupt changes are his trigger. Therefore, we are always employing a variety of strategies, so switching tasks will be less traumatic for all of us. We have found you can use something as simple as a deck of playing cards to smooth out the switches. A card with a number 5, any suit, will let Ed know, you have five minutes before we switch. You could also use a card with a 10, any suit, and Ed would know he has a ten-minute warning. We simply place a single card in his hand, and Ed is silently informed a transition is coming. You can also use other tactile objects like colored poker chips. Colors often associated with movement like red, yellow, and green is a good place to start. The chips, like the cards, offer a verbal and visual prompt, as well as a tactile reminder. The tactile reminder keeps Ed present in the upcoming transition, instead of staying self-absorbed in whatever else he was doing previously. If you think about it, red represents "stop what you are doing and get ready for a change". Then, yellow is "ramp up your engine", and finally. green means "let's go".

Either method, playing cards or red, yellow, and green chips, can easily be dropped or placed into his hand, or an agreed upon clear container or clear plastic bag. The tactile reminders prepare Ed for the shift and significantly diminish his anxieties.

The Gift of Song

There was another strategy we adopted that has been proven to be controversial for some families; giving your child a phone. We did our research and were fully aware of all the risks that come with a phone connected to the internet. We justified our decision because Ed's attachment issues were drastically diminished when he was able to text his Mom or

Dad to verify our location. Even if we are all in the house at the same time, Ed relaxes better when he knows where we are. Such an easy task brings him frequent comfort. What we have come to understand, Ed's biological mother gifted him with attachment issues and a fear that others might forget or abandon him. However, God has gifted Ed something else, a beautiful singing voice. As we groom his vocal talents, Ed continually needs access to music to learn lyrics and to hear a variety of songs his vocal coach recommends. This serves as one more reason to have access to his own phone. A camera to record his progress, and for us to view, has proven beneficial as well. His vocal gift has given him new confidence, and it lowers his anxiety when he sings and dances. In fact, we have been blessed to watch Ed perform in about ten musicals with our local community theater. We can now imagine such a bright future for our son.

Transitions are far less traumatic for Ed if we all use the strategies we have learned. With his 504 plan, and recently an IEP, Ed can utilize the accommodations that are in place to help him be more successful and less stressed at school. Music and dance have given him more confidence as Ed navigates his world and lives in a home where no one will abandon him. Ed adores his older brother, Evan. However, on a few occasions, he strongly hinted he would like a brother closer to his own age.

IO

HARLEY'S OFF AT SCHOOL

Harley Ray's story began before we ever set eyes on him. Before we even realized we were existing and surviving on the same planet.

On or about April 25, 2015, Harley sustained a serious injury. Harley is a curious child but does not always anticipate that somethings, or someone, could harm him. At some point in the evening, Harley found a torch lighter and some other drug paraphernalia that had been left unattended. Not understanding how the torch worked, Harley accidentally lit his shirt on fire. Harley's shrieking woke the people in the apartment.

What happened next, has been pieced together by reports from Harley's older brother, the police, and the first responders.

What Deb and I came to realize later was that his older brother took a picture of Harley's injuries and sent that photo to his biological mother. Why? Because their father refused to get medical help for Harley. Grasping his father's obstinance, Harley's brother posted to his Facebook and his mother called 911 from another state.

When the Glendale Police arrived at the apartment, Harley's father and the girlfriend were not present. Harley was observed to be naked, lying on the floor on a sheet with serious injuries. The medical report indicated a six-year-old white male sustained second and third-degree burns over twenty percent of his body. Many of the injuries were on this left side, up and down his rib cage, as well as the upper portion of his hip and his left arm. Harley was immediately transported to the Arizona Burn Center at Maricopa Medical.

According to the police report, Harley's father stated he was not in the home at the time of the incident, and he heard about the accident from his roommate. The roommate was typically left in charge of the children when the father was not home. In either case, the ambulance was never called by the father, the girlfriend, or by the father's roommate.

However, in a later interview, the father stated he was in the home at the time of the incident. He also stated that he had no idea the burns were as severe as the medical professionals had discovered. This was his explanation for why he did not call the emergency personnel. The reason he was not at home when the police arrived was because they had gone to the store to buy bandages and ointment to apply to the burns. He further asserted that he had intended to take his son to the hospital after applying the ointment. His delayed reaction was because he was hindered by a seizure and could not drive his son to the emergency room.

According to the report, all adults in the home had not handled the emergency appropriately. The brother and the roommate reported that the father and his girlfriend were sleeping at the home during the incident. It was further reported that the father had changed his recollection of the events several times. As a result, an investigator was assigned to the case. According to the investigator, the patient's brother reportedly called authorities in the past where he had described his father as abusive. There were additional allegations that the father and his girlfriend could have been using marijuana during the supervision of Harley and the incident. The brother noted that no one was willing or able to be assigned as guardians to take care of them. The investigator learned the patient was reportedly diagnosed with autism although Harley has never received services. The patient's father was arrested for medical neglect.

I Couldn't Leave Him There

This is when we joined Harley's story — after he went to the Arizona Burn Center. We received a call from Child Protective Services asking us to foster Harley after he was released from the hospital. We were caring for a thirteen-year-old boy at the time and did not have an empty bed. However, if our thirteen-year-old was returned to his biological family and that would probably happen, we would certainly consider it.

Because the next months were consumed with court appearances and ordered visits for the thirteen-year-old as he transitioned back home; Deb had prayed often about the request from CPS. When the call came again, it signaled something deep inside Deb's busy brain as she recalled a story of a little boy who had been badly burned. Deb also remembered he had already experienced a bizarre life and a history of abuse and neglect was already a big part of Harley's past. We had previously heard the scattered details of the April 25th incident and there was a new element; his biological mother's parental rights had been terminated after she had placed Harley in a washing machine to clean him up. CPS needed us to understand, if we agreed to foster Harley, he would require wound care, and he would need to wear a special garment for his burns for one year. Harley would have to go to the burn center once per week to receive burn treatment and occupational therapy. CPS understood this was a big ask, but after reviewing a collection of favorable reports as foster parents, they were praying we would say, yes.

There was a standing joke at my office when people heard stories about our fostering ministry. People would ask, "Kevin, how many kids do you have?" I would say, "When I left this morning, I had three." Knowing Deb's heart was as big as the Grand Canyon, that number was subject to change depending on the availability of beds or cribs, and how many times CPS called her in a day. Four months had gone by, and we had an empty bed, so Deb agreed to go to the Burn Center to chat with the nurses about Harley and gauge the time commitment he would require. Stefy had her own set of daily demands, so Deb was going to determine if she could manage her, as well as the trips expected by the Burn Center. A quick peck on the cheek and reminder for Deb to just learn about his treatment plan was all she needed to accomplish that day. So, I was not I surprised when I received a text and photo of a blond-haired blue-eyed boy buckled in my wife's car with a lovely smile even though his left arm was all wrapped in gauze. The text read, "I know, I know, but I couldn't leave him there."

Harley's arrival immediately resulted in numerous events: frequent visits to the burn center, fittings for a new wound garment, meetings with numerous doctors to order meds, then adjust meds, pink eye, eye exams, bifocal glasses, ear infections, lice, constipation, toilet training, enrollment in a local school, IEP meetings, psychological evaluation, purchasing another bike, and training wheels.

The medical visits were routine, remarkably similar to each of our new foster placements. However, the behavioral aspect soon became a distinguishable and daily challenge. Harley would be seven in May, because of his childish behaviors, we strongly believed he had never seen the inside of a preschool or any kind of school. When we reached out to his case manager, Deb and I finally confirmed what we had already anticipated. Harley had never attended a preschool or Kindergarten.

The case manager informed us that some type of academic testing had been attempted while in the hospital. Sadly, Harley was unable to complete any portions of the achievement tests. At six years old, Harley did not easily recognize letters or numbers by sight. He only knew a couple of letter names and Harley could not count. Happily, Harley was able to write the letter H, when asked to print out his name. When he was asked if there were other letters for his name, Harley just wrote the letter H over and over and over.

In addition, we realized that Harley's speech and language appeared to be significantly delayed. He continually used repetitive sounds in place of words. There were many times we would ask him to slow down so we could better understand what he was saying, and this just made Harley frustrated or irritated.

Attempt Number One

Socially, Harley appeared to have extremely unsafe boundaries. It did not matter where we were, Harley would not wait for us to tell people his name before he was wrapping them in a bear hug. When we were out in public, if we did not keep track of him every minute, we would just follow the nearest "Oh My!" or "Careful little man!" and we'd find Harley wrapped around a stranger. We had been told that Harley frequently touched members of the hospital staff without warning as well. Basically, Harley did not appear to have any awareness of socially appropriate behavior. He may appear as sweet, but most people were extremely uncomfortable with his ignorance of personal boundaries. This became very apparent when we enrolled him in Kindergarten at our neighborhood school.

When we checked in with Harley's teacher a few days later, she reported that Harley was a loving, kind, and joyful. She believed Harley liked being in her classroom. Interestingly, Harley's teacher noticed his behaviors to be more reflective of a two or three-year-old; rather than a Kindergartner. Finally, she shared that Harley often wandered around the room and got into things.

By the end of Harley's second week, her nurturing tone and demeanor had truly transformed. This time Harley's teacher hastily conveyed that Harley was resistant towards sitting and participating and often did not respond to words such as "no" or "stop", especially on the playground. There were times when Harley would push all the crayons off the table and refuse to pick them up. He would also push over stacks of paper and make other large messes in the classroom. Harley had the most difficulty with showing and understanding other people's personal space. His touching, poking, or pinching the other students made many of them upset.

Harley's teacher looked exhausted as she further described how she was currently working on teaching Harley how to raise his hand in the classroom and to walk through the hallway without talking or touching anyone. Her strategy was to hold his hand as the class walked through the hallways. She gave one massive sigh and then finished her final thoughts, "Harley has been having a lot of bathroom accidents at school."

Mercifully for this teacher, Harley's first run at Kindergarten quickly came to an end in her classroom a few days later, when he put his hands on one of his female classmates. The father of the little girl he choked threatened to sue the school if Harley was allowed back into the school. This choking incident resulted in the sudden formation of a crisis team for Harley and a quick transfer to another school within the district. This team apparently had more experience with Harley's behaviors as well as his lack of academics.

After a few days, Deb and I were summoned for our first meeting with his new crisis team. They were all very professional and well prepared as they began reciting their collection of observations.

The first member of their team began, "Harley is currently in foster placement. Harley is exhibiting major struggles academically, socially, and behaviorally." Our first thought; their initial notations are all accurate and we off to an honest start.

Then a member of the crisis team testified Harley became overly stimulated easily and required redirection timeouts from staff to become calm. Her explanation centered on the need for social connection and attention. The staff member felt the behavioral techniques she was utilizing would help manage his behaviors.

The next member jumped in with excitement in her voice, "Harley has demonstrated some severe emotional outbursts, including hitting other children. Harley is very far behind academically, verbally, and socially. This is will likely be a source of considerable frustration for Harley. He will continue to feel overwhelmed in the mainstream classroom." Collectively, the team recommended, as Harley's guardians, we should pursue educational services immediately. There was no question that Harley would be eligible for and in much need of such services.

Our joint journey as Harley's primary educational advocates began. With numerous notes from all his medical visits in hand, we knew what lay ahead. Deb and I would need to repeat his story over and over and over as we met with each of the services that he would become eligible for.

From doctor's office to doctor's office, from school office to school office, Deb and I sounded like a broken record as we began telling Harley's story: "At home, Harley is fun and lovable; he adores people and wants to be friends with everyone. Harley is not aggressive at home. He is cooperative with daily routines. Sadly, Harley wets the bed every night."

When we were asked about Harley's academics we shared, "We have noticed that Harley has significant difficulty learning. Based on our observations Harley does not retain concepts like colors, letters, or any social behavioral cues. According to his many medical specialists, they attribute his difficulties as a result of fetal alcohol syndrome."

Next, we would continue with Harley's physical concerns. Deb or I disclosed that we had been worried about his eyesight, so we had him tested. Harley was prescribed glasses. He needed trifocals for one eye, and bifocals for the other. Harley also had a mild hearing loss and his doctor believed this was a residual effect from ongoing ear infections and should not impede his daily living.

Now that he was in school, it was reported that Harley demonstrated aggressive behaviors, was easily distracted, cried when denied his own way, babbled to himself, and had a very short attention span. His teachers also told us that Harley was easily annoyed by others, threatens others, and shows feelings that do not fit the situation.

We knew that Harley changes his moods quickly and acts without thinking. We had seen Harley stare blankly as if others are not there. He said things that make no sense. Simply put, Harley had poor self-control and we noticed he had trouble keeping his balance. The school confirmed this when they sent home reports letting us know that Harley falls easily.

Deb and I learned what worried the people at this school more than anything else was that Harley lost his temper without warning and lashed out. His teachers had observed Harley going up to classmates' desks and knocking off pencils, papers, and markers. According to the lead teacher, she guessed that the team would discover that Harley would have general delays in all domains of behavioral functioning.

After everyone had shared, the team requested that we sign off on testing. With so many issues to process, we were happy to sign.

Weeks later, after all his psychological, academic, and behavioral assessments were completed, Deb and I were beckoned back by the former crisis crew, now caringly referred to as "Harley's Academic Team."

To summarize their findings: Due to his limited attention span and physical aggression, Harley would require constant supervision in a small group or one-on-one settings. The academic team was extremely concerned that a very large portion of classroom time was spent by the teacher redirecting his behaviors. These behaviors would be too much for one teacher. In short, Harley was a handful. Harley would need a new classroom setting.

Attempt Number Two

We had received some grace while the testing was finalized, but just like Kindergarten, we eventually got the disheartening call from his new principal. She spoke quickly and firmly, "At school today, your child, Harley, required the use of timeout and restraint. Harley became upset when he did not want to listen to the group story and started yelling. He was then moved to a de-escalation area in the classroom where he tried to knock over a bookshelf. Harley began to hit the substitute teacher on the arm and the substitute paraprofessional notified another teacher who then transported Harley to the timeout room. Upon arrival in timeout, Harley started hitting and kicking the substitute teacher. The substitute teacher notified other staff members who reported to the timeout room. Restraint was used for 15 minutes because Harley was continuing to hit, bite, and kick staff.

Once he was calm, Harley was able to walk back to class by himself and sat on the carpet during singing time. Harley began to hit students and was quickly moved away from the other students. As the principal, I was called back to the room where I sat with Harley on the carpet. Harley then tried to hit me as I tried to calm him down. Because it was determined that Harley was not safe, he cannot ride the bus home. We are contacting you to come pick him up. Harley was seen by the nurse; no injuries were detected. A debriefing meeting will be held today after school to discuss his behaviors. If you have any further questions, please reach out and contact us." By the tone of her voice, we knew the wheels were already in motion to relocate Harley to another school. He had made it to the end of May, but we were certain Harley would not be allowed to return to his second attempt at school.

During his end of the year IEP meeting, the team did determine Harley would be eligible for ESY, Extended School Year. When Harley attended the ESY summer session, his new teacher wrote, "Harley really enjoyed being a helper and I tried to let him help whenever possible. For example, Harley helped me run the smartboard. I found that, when we were doing group activities, if Harley did not want to work, he was able to clearly tell me he just did not want to do it. We find it is best to let Harley pick the tasks he wants to complete first. Once, he was practicing letters and did not want to identify them anymore. Harley asked me if he could choose other work. We think he likes to be in control of his choices. As long as he does the work, we are okay if he is in control of the sequence. Harley appears to be upbeat and positive about our suggestions. Sometimes, Harley likes to remind me to give him the reward he earned before it is time to go home."

Our thoughts were that this teacher had connected with Harley. She continued to report positive experiences with Harley, "A few minutes before the bus arrived to take him home, Harley told me that he wanted his mom to pick him up. I merely responded that I bet he likes it when mom picks him up, but that mom was expecting him to come home on the bus. Then I asked him what he thought Mom would say if he did not want to go on the bus today. Harley just smiled at me, that was the end of it. Each time, Harley waved goodbye as he grabbed his backpack and got on the bus. I always try to let Harley know when transitions are going to be happening. I tell him that he can do one more thing and then it will be time to change. This really helps. I hope Harley is enjoying his summer. If you have any questions, do not hesitate to contact me." A summer with this teacher and the ESY program encouraged

Deb and me to move forward with a new site for Harley's third attempt at school.

Other life events that had occurred as well were encouraging. On April 25, 2016, Harley's biological father signed a consent to place his child up for adoption where he relinquished his rights. On July 13, 2016, Harley's biological mother signed a consent to place the child up for adoption and relinquished her rights. In December of 2017, we were given the green light to adopt Harley.

Attempt Number Three

Harley was nine years old when he began his third attempt at school. We were enjoying a few months of grace in Harley's third educational setting. However, when he was assigned another new teacher, our honeymoon period was over; Harley's old behaviors resurfaced. His new teacher felt Harley was impulsive and had a very short attention span. Each day we would read notes that Harley struggled to stay on task when working with everyone or small groups. His new teacher did determine that Harley could work best when it was one-on-one, but this school could not provide that option since the class was already so small, with only eight boys. They did provide one behavior coach, but he would be working with all the students throughout the school.

Harley began running away from adults when he was asked to sit or transition to another area. Harley began copying other students' inappropriate behaviors. His teacher reported that Harley hit himself in the head when he appeared unhappy or upset. There were times he pulled his own hair when frustrated. Mostly, Harley was physically aggressive towards other students and adults by pinching or hitting anyone who was standing or sitting near him. Harley was given verbal reminders to keep his hands to himself. If this was ineffective, then the behavior coach was notified, and he was removed from the situation. When this happened, Harley got more upset and behaviors escalated. Harley would slap, punch, kick, bite, pinch, scratch, or head butt. He yelled loudly, threw his shoes or his glasses, and licked objects near him when he was upset. Because most of Harley's classmates demonstrated similar behaviors, a large portion of classroom time was spent by redirecting and requesting behavioral support. With all that said, his teacher wanted us to know the amount of academic instruction was limited. Each time Deb visited the school, she felt like the teacher and the behavior coach were always putting out behavioral fires.

Harley's third attempt at school was spiraling out of control. At the end of the year, Deb and I requested a meeting with the head of the Special Education department for the school district. We simply asked if we could revisit a school, one we had toured a year earlier but did not choose because of the distance.

Our tour was conducted by the school principal, who we did not meet with the first time we toured. Deb and I were extremely encouraged by what we heard and saw. As we drove home, we both knew this setting would be a better choice for Harley.

Attempt Number Four

Harley had already been scheduled for reconstructive improvement surgery for his upper left arm in early August. This operation would smooth out some rough, thick scar tissue resulting from his burns. The timing was ideal, Harley could start their ESY program in late July, have his surgery, recover at home during the school's summer break, and then start with a new team in the middle of August. When Harley announced his arrival home after his first day, we noticed something immediately. Harley was not frustrated, angry, or exhausted.

Was it possible? Could Harley's fourth attempt at school start positive and stay positive?

We did not hear from Harley's new school team for most of August. Deb received a daily email from his teacher with a rating for academics and behaviors. It was fairly basic; a 1 was good, a 0 meant improvements needed. The emails were mostly a collection of 1's. We received no phone calls. We adopted the saying; no news is good news. Then in September, we were asked to update his Individual Education Plan, IEP. Deb and I sat down around a large oval wooden table with their team of five specialists. Each participant was well prepared and delivered their detailed observations. I was writing down their thoughts as quickly as I could.

To summarize, their comments went something like this: "Harley is a 10-year-old 4th grader. He is a kind, friendly young man with a sweet smile and a great sense of humor. Harley is always willing to work hard, even on tasks that are difficult for him. Harley is able to independently initiate interactions with peers by joining activities such as playing with LEGOS, kinetic sand, and/or playing with classroom toys. Harley prides himself on his independent nature. He is eager to participate in classroom activities such as leading calendar and passing out class materials. Harley does best when given a multi-sensory approach to learning and thrives when given positive reinforcement. Harley benefits from a lot of verbal praise for good work throughout the day. He excels in a highly structured environment, working in small groups, and a low student to staff ratio. Harley is more motivated in completing academic tasks when provided with the opportunity to earn highly preferred incentives and utilizing a token system. Furthermore, Harley performs his absolute best when given the opportunity to develop a rapport with staff."

Deb and I looked at each other in awe and wonder. They were describing the boy that we were living with, not the angry child that attempted school time after time and failed.

His new team members clearly covered his social, emotional, and behavioral goals and expectations with care and expertise. His nurturing and well-seasoned teacher explained, in exceptional detail, his academic achievements accurately, and provided an analysis of his learning characteristics that predicted academic successes. Overall, it was a well-executed, comprehensive plan that gave Deb and I something we were looking for with Harley; Hope.

Yes, there had always been a honeymoon period with each attempt, but Harley's fourth attempt at this school was different. Harley was coming home every day thrilled to share what had transpired at school. Most importantly, Harley was not taking naps for an hour or two after he got home. Because he would sleep at school and at home, we could tell Harley was experiencing frustration, rage, and anxiety at his former attempts at school.

After four long, exasperating years and a half dozen exhausted, stressed out classroom teachers, behavior coaches, and specialists; Harley was settling into his home away from home. Harley could finally relax and be still. We have only seen these results in Harley in one other setting, Camp Courage.

Camp Courage is run through the Arizona Burn Foundation. Typically held in the early part of June, Camp Courage was created to address the emotional needs of children who have suffered severe burn injuries. Their primary purpose of the foundation is to assist burn survivors and their families from crisis to recovery, to a thriving life, one day at a time. Harley is a boy of few words, but when I asked him why he likes camp so much, he replied, "They make me feel happy and loved! I get so excited when I think about all the activities we get to do!" Camp Courage and his new school mean the world to Harley.

Harley's way with words has provided his mom and dad with some huge smiles and numerous chuckles on certain occasions. His quirky wit comes out at the perfect time recapping the situation he finds himself in. His favorite sayings are,

"That was awkward!", "We'll See." or "Oh, Well." Harley has such a tender heart that when bad news comes his way, he takes it hard. In the summer of 2020, we had to tell our cognitively challenged Harley that his biological father had died unexpectedly. It was difficult for him to comprehend, and by default, Harley can no longer threaten us that he wants to go live with his old dad. The courts had already finalized that. Harley never could see him again. Now his mysterious death made that truly final. Harley can never use that baseless suggestion again because I am his only dad. However, when it comes to the important people in Harley's life, I take a back seat to his favorite person to chat with, his biological brother, Howard.

II

OH HOWARD

You cannot fully understand Harley's story unless you come to know his brothers' story as well. Shortly after Harley arrived, our case manager reminded us that Harley had a sixteen-year-old sibling; a brother named, Howard. He was currently living in a group home and was asking his case manager many questions about these people who became Harley's new placement. Howard had visited Harley as often as they would let him go to the hospital; the case manager mentioned he was very protective of his little brother. In fact, we learned he was the primary caretaker for Harley, even though several adults were living with them at the time of Harley's accident. Howard's Facebook post was the catalyst that alerted his family, who then notified the police and first responders.

Our current foster placement, a thirteen-year-old boy, was transitioning back home with his birth mother. According to the courts, his birth mom had satisfactorily accomplished all the tasks required of her. The courts felt it was time for this thirteen-year-old to move home. Our 20-month roller-coaster ride of a placement was coming to an end. As customary for foster parents, we had presented each of our concerns to the Foster Care Review Board and to his assigned Guardian Ad

Litem or court-appointed special advocate (CASA). The judge would hear all the recommendations and make the final decision. We were certain this socially awkward boy, with an incredibly low IQ, who had suffered severe physical and verbal abuse at the hands of his biological father was moving back home. His persistent fascination with pornography led us to believe he had been a victim of sexual abuse or had witnessed firsthand the abuse of his female siblings. With such a troublesome past, their current housing and sleeping areas for three teenagers were still not finalized, yet all indications from the court tipped toward a favorable reunification.

We had built a new home to better accommodate our foster and adopted kids, as well as an aging parent. The last night before the scheduled move, our foster son asked me if he could go say goodnight to Stefy. He was always gentle with Stefy, even from the first day he moved in, so I agreed and went back down the hall of the apartment we were renting. I had only been sitting in the living room a few minutes when a voice inside told me to look for him. I did not find him in his room or the boy's bathroom. I walked back down the hallway and opened the door to Stefy's room and there he was. He was on Stefy's bed, she was lying on her stomach in front of him. He was on her bed behind her, on his knees. He had his athletic shorts and underwear pulled down, and he was visibly aroused. I quickly scanned the bed again to see that Stefy was sound asleep under her blanket. Not wanting to wake her, I strongly spoke his first name and told him to leave Stefy's room. I could feel my heart beating wildly in my chest. I checked Stefy once again, still asleep. I gave her a brief kiss on the forehead, prayed I could stay calm. I went back down the hall to our foster son's bedroom, taking deep calming breaths with every step.

He was on his bed, sobbing. He hastily apologized and told me that he did not do anything. He did not hurt Stefy. I do not even want to think about what would have happened if I had opened the door one minute later. What if I had not inter-rupted an unpleasant incident from happening to our non-verbal daughter? Even though I wanted to put this young man against the wall and thrash him, my heart reminded me he was already a victim of abuse. He did not choose the life he had been hurled into. After I calmed him down, I put him to bed. I gave him strict orders, "Do not leave this room until morning!" Then, I closed the door to his room. I already knew the evening was just getting started.

I spent the next few hours first calling Deb; she was already at work. I had rapidly told Deb what had happened, then agreed we would talk more when she got home. Next, I had to call Child Protective Services, and then our case manager to report the incident. Both asked if we needed a crisis inter-vention team sent out to remove our placement. Both times, I said, "No." As much as I wanted to protect my daughter, I also knew if our foster son was removed in the middle of the night, the reunification with his family would be null and void. After Deb came home, I replayed the incident all over again and the subsequent conversations. Deb and I assured each other we would report everything to the judge, his Guardian Ad Litem, the FCRB, begging all of them to ensure this mixed-up young man would receive court-ordered sexual abuse counseling.

The week we moved into our new home, we had a secu-rity system installed to notify us if anyone entered Stefy's room after we put her to bed or down for a nap. The alarm on our bedroom monitor would also sound if our foster son left his room after we sent him to bed. With that accom-plished, we took one long, deep breath; in a few weeks, he would be reunited with his birth mom and some of his sib-lings. We stayed vigilant right up to the last minute before he left. In the court's final decision, he could return home under the condition that every family member received sexual abuse counseling.

Just Not Yet

With that difficult season behind us, we still had to address Howard's question about his request to see his brother more, now that he was out of the hospital. Deb and I were not ready to jump right in the court-ordered visitation pool this soon, especially with another teenage boy. We asked our case manager if she had any case histories that would give us a clue to Howard's past. We hoped and felt we had a right to know before we consented to brotherly visits. We were only allowed a glimpse at a few public-school records. Deb and I were not encouraged by what we read.

We learned that Howard came into care the same day that Harley had his accident. Howard was admitted to a group home on April 27, 2015. While in the group home, Howard did attend a charter school, and this group compiled as much information on him as they could. First, they learned Howard attended school in Oklahoma up until fifth grade, then he transferred to a school in Arizona. He transferred to another school in 2011 and enrolled there as a seventh-grader. While in school, we read Howard had been given a 504 plan in Oklahoma, but he never received special education services. During his seventh-grade year, the new school team decided to conduct an evaluation on Howard and qualified him under the category of an emotional disability. He moved on from junior high and enrolled in a high school in Arizona as a freshman. Somehow, Howard attended his ninth and tenth-grade year identified as a student with an emotional disability.

Beyond his school attendance and spotty academic record, this team also recovered some behavioral information. According to their findings, Howard's developmental history was uneventful and could be considered typical for his age. However, his father stated that Howard began to display abnormal behaviors around the age of three; when he allegedly tried to microwave a cat. Since that time, Howard had been known to be obsessed with guns, knives, and fire.

At this time, Howard claimed to be hearing voices as well, had mood swings, including violent episodes of anger. He apparently cried for no obvious reason and refused to eat. Previous statements provided by his birth father claimed Howard had been diagnosed with a bipolar disorder, psychosis, an anxiety disorder, and finally, a learning disorder. His biological father also reported that Howard had a history of more than one suicide attempt. The case manager could not locate any medical records indicating Howard had seen a doctor, but his biological father stated that Howard was taking Risperidone, Lithium, and Hydroxyzine. However, the group home never received any prescribed medications and reported Howard did not appear to be a threat to himself or to others.

Next, the new charter school, associated with the group home, administered an intelligence test. This assessment found Howard to be well within the average range both verbally and nonverbally. Academically, Howard presented with adequate mathematical skills, but poor language arts skills. When Howard arrived at the group home, he was angry about his situation. His erratic emotions were not a surprise to us when his case manager indicated he had behavioral difficulties at school that led to frequent classroom disruptions and office referrals. Overall, the group home and the school agreed Howard had an emotional disability that interfered with his ability to be successful at school and would require special education services; a modified curriculum, assistance with language arts, small group instruction, and close monitoring for his unpredictable behavior. His crisis intervention team believed Howard's current emotional instability impaired his ability to form meaningful and lasting relationships with his peers and did not allow him to control his thoughts or feelings under normal circumstances. All their findings helped us better understand his pervasive mood of unhappiness, resulting in his failing grades.

That was a lot of information to take in. A lot. After processing all that we learned, we went back and looked again at what was reported to be fact and what was more likely fiction. We saw a pattern of what his birth father described, appeared to be more fictional than factual. We did not want to keep these brothers apart, but with the background info we had just gathered, Deb and I were not in a hurry to rush visitations. Yet we knew in our hearts, prolonged separations would not be fair to Harley. As suggested by their case manager, we agreed to visitations where a driver would pick up the boys from our home and take them to see their birth dad. This quickly became the pattern of our weekends. This became the new us.

Howard would arrive from the group home with a driver, pick up Harley, and off they would go for visitations with their birth dad. By the time Howard approached Deb and me with an idea, he had been at the group home for over six months. From side conversations we had with him before and after his dad visits, Howard knew our former foster kid had moved on. Howard wanted us to know, he was ready to leave the group home and was hoping to move in with us and to be closer to his little brother. I did not answer right away because I was not ready to commit to Howard's request. He was already 16, in a couple of short years, he would age out of the foster care system. Howard had witnessed some things that children should never be exposed to. I was not convinced he would be a good fit for our house. However, Deb and I cautiously agreed to commit to a trial run of a weekend overnight. Extra insight from his group home supervisors gave us a little hope; after being with them for a few months, Howard had started asking for help on a more regular basis when needed. He was putting more effort into his school performance as well. He was able to be redirected and utilized cooldown periods and opportunities to work in small groups and individual settings.

Howard's overnight weekends played out in a typical honeymoon fashion. Howard's demeanor was well-mannered and courteous. He was on his best behavior every minute he was in our home. So, I had to ask him, "Howard, you will probably age out of the system at eighteen. In less than two years, you will have a chance to really be on your own, with some financial support from the foster care system. You seem to be doing so well in the group home and your school. Why, Howard? Why would you want to come out here and live with us? We are old people, not a young couple. We do not play video games, watch sports, or eat out all the time. Howard, we are not, I repeat, *not*, exciting people."

Howard has always had an irresistible smile. When he turns it on, you cannot help but smile, too. He looked at both of us and said, "I really, really want to be with my brother. I am so done with living in a group home. I just want to be a part of a family." Damn, this kid knew how to schmooze. Regrettably, this was a skillset, a tool his birth father used to make connections, gain favors, and then conduct his dubious business dealings. So, when Howard turns on his smile and the "Howie" schmooze comes, you are drawn in. Like an accident on the highway, you cannot turn away; you are pulled in by his words and his grin. You cannot help but ask yourself, "where is this going? What does he really want?"

We clearly heard what Howard wanted, to be a junior in a brick and mortar school. For a normalized sixteen-year-old, that might be feasible. I knew high school students in Arizona needed a minimum of 22 credits in their core academic subjects to earn a diploma. Howard was more worried about whether he would have to suddenly leave a school, not if he had earned any credits. He remembered taking some classes but was not sure if he stayed in the school long enough to earn any grades or credits. With a little detective work, I was able to find nine earned credits; including those he had just earned while living at his group home.

We began our school search by visiting three high schools in the area to learn what they could do for Howard. Two institutions offered him online restorative classes. Only one met with us and proposed the following schedules. In his first year, as a junior, just like he wanted, he was expected to take the following required classes: (1) Construction Technology, (2) Geometry (3) Algebra I Foundations (4) Human Anatomy and Physiology (5) English Literature 9, (6) English World Literature 10, (7) World History, and (8) Theater. That grouping would be his junior year. If he passed each of those classes, the school counselor proposed this schedule for his senior year. Howard would take and need to pass a second set of full credit and half-credit required courses: (1) PE, (2) English and British Literature 11 (3) Algebra II, (4) Economics, (5) English IV (6) English IV Support (7) Consumer Math and (8) Civics and Government. There were no variations allowed, this young man would not see a study hall or a free period for two years. In my career as an educator, this tight schedule would make any high schooler cringe.

I told Howard that based on what we knew about foster kids his age, the statistics were not in his favor. Most males in foster care did not finish high school, let alone get a high school diploma. I promised Howard, "If you work hard, follow the schedule, earn the grades, earn the credits, and no deviations; it could be done." I vowed not to let Howard be a statistic.

The next few months were a whirlwind of adjustments; adapting to homework, struggling with study skills, driving lessons, managing his first phone, as well as location sharing, dating curfews, picking out appropriate Prom clothing, resume writing, job hunting, and car shopping. I am not going to tell anyone it was easy, but Howard agreed to it all. First, we updated his IEP. I wanted him to have any advantages that he could. With his IEP, Howard could request some pull out time to work in a small group setting, to minimize distractions by peers, and to focus on controlling behaviors. Fast forward, Howard finished his junior year, earning all seven of the credits while maintaining a B plus average.

That accomplishment was impressive for a young man who had been living a precarious, complicated life with his birth father. Then along came this guy who promised to help him to earn a diploma. The difference, I put Howard first. And I was going to keep my promise. As he began his senior year in August, I maintained ongoing contact with the school. I could easily have been labeled a helicopter, a bulldozer, or a drone parent. The parent everybody talks about, not always in a positive way. I did not earn that title because Captain Howie schmoozed his way through his final year of high school. Howard always knew which teachers to schmooze and manipulate, to win over, and to bring value to his situation. One teacher told me, "Howard eventually hands in all his assignments, but often takes his phone out, usually at the beginning of class. He will put it away when he is told." She just had to tell him a lot. "Howard turns in most homework, but easily gets off task during group assignments. He is too social most of the time."

Other teachers told us, "Howard's weaknesses are that he is too chatty. Howard loves to talk and often does not listen because he thinks he knows what he is doing and therefore misses new material. Howard is very respectful but talks too much. When I asked him to stop, he will apologize, he will smile at you, but then he goes back to talking. He is a joy to teach in his construction class. He often takes charge of small group projects. When Howard is determined, there is nothing that gets in his way. However, he can get off task easily and sometimes has a hard time following directions or orders." Nevertheless, he charmed his way through his senior year and earned the rest of the credits and his high school diploma.

There was more to Howard than being a student. He did have a life outside of school. As with many of our foster children, Deb kept a log of their day to day, week to week, or month to month milestones. She recorded when Howard got his driver's license and when he landed his first job at an arcade and bowling alley. We talked to him about saving some of his paychecks for a car. That was hard for Howard because he loved hanging out with his guy friends, going to the movies, and playing video games when he was not working. Howard and I went to the movies quite frequently. In fact, I have a framed collection of all the ticket stubs for the movies we saw in those first two years of his arrival. It was during the movies that he first called me "Kevy," and I returned the favor and nicknamed him "Howie." The movie theater was a place where we made that guy connection, sitting next to each other in a theater. I remember during the previews, he would tap me and say, "Kevy, let's go see that one. Kevy, let's go see that one. Kevy, let's go see that one." You know, we probably did. It was something Howie and Kevy did together almost every Friday night.

Just Harley?

In Howard's senior year, we were informed by the courts that Harley was available for adoption. So, one morning, Deb told Howard we were planning on adopting Harley. Deb said Howard took one look at her and said two words, "Just Harley?" After I heard about his response, I challenged him again, "Howard, you're almost 18. Very soon, you can legally be on your own. Why would you want a couple of old farts to adopt you?"

What is vastly different having a foster son who is 16 is that he came along to all the court dates and Foster Care Review Board meetings. We never needed to prep him; Howard always spoke to these adults with his heart. He would explain to board members, case managers, and judges why it was important for him to be with his brother, why he didn't want to live with his biological father, why the people who took him in believed in him and believed that he could accomplish whatever he wanted to do. Whenever we went to court, the judge would often ask to just speak to Howard alone in his chambers. Howard would just tell us later; he just told the judge he did not want to go back to his dad. He wanted to be with Deb and me.

On November 22, 2016, Howard signed off on this statement saying, "I Howard Max Dale, want Kevin and Deb Sieling to adopt me and be my parents. I know that Kevin and Deb Sieling will be my only parents. This means that no one, but Kevin and Deb Sieling will have to provide me with a place to live, food to eat, clothing, money, or anything else I may need. This consent is signed by me freely and voluntarily without any fraud, duress, coercion, or undue influence. I am acting of sound mind. I want to be adopted and my name to be changed to Howard Max Dale Sieling."

Howie had a big year. By the time he turned 18, Howie and his little brother were adopted, Howie was a licensed driver, a wage earner, and a high school graduate. Those were big adjustments but what never changed was his impulsive nature.

Mr. Impulsive

We received a glimpse into his chaotic future on October 25, sixteen days after he moved in with us. Howard was playing tag at the park with his little brothers and our grandkids. He decided to avoid being tagged by jumping from the top of a fifteen-foot-high playground structure. Howie landed on both feet, but not gracefully, and he broke his ankle. So, sixteen days after he came into our home, Howie was already in a cast.

When Howie had finally saved up $600 dollars, we told him we would match what he had saved for his first car. So, Howie scoured the internet and finally landed on a vehicle he thought would be a good buy and one he could afford. It was listed at $1,200. After he showed Deb all the details on his phone, Deb suggested that we all go together to look at the car as a family. On the way there, I repeatedly reminded Howie to not come across as too anxious, too impulsive. When we located the owner of the car in the parking lot, Howard and this total stranger took it for a test drive. As they pulled away, I noticed a cracked windshield, paint chipping off the hood, the trunk, and the side panels, plus all four tires looked bald. While they circled the block, I could not help but notice a huge spot of fresh oil on the ground where the car had been parked.

When they returned, I took Howard off to the side and said, "Listen, Bud," and I pointed out everything, the broken windshield, the bald tires, the dripping oil, the body of the car. Remember, you can always negotiate the price, you can go back and forth, point out some of the flaws, you got this?" Howard nodded with affirmation as he walked back over to the guy. He sauntered up to the guy and questioned, "So, how much were you asking for the car again?" and the guy said "1,200 dollars" In my opinion, it was a ridiculous price for this car. Howard points to the vehicle and cautiously says, "I noticed that the windshield is cracked. I see all the tires are old. I will probably have to replace all of them. I think it's leaking oil." The guy actually smirks at Howie and states, "Yep, it's all true. So kid, what would you think?" The guy looked at Howie, shrugs his shoulders, and says, "How about $1,100?" Impulsive Howie, thrusts out his hand, grabs the guys hand, and shakes on it, "Deal!"

We kept our promise and gave Howie the $600.00 we agreed on. I followed Deb and Howie home. I was not sure the car would even make the 30-minute drive back to our house. Later, Deb drove it to a local licensed auto mechanic and had it assessed. The estimate of repairs for his first lemon would be between $2,000 to $3,000. Someone from our church suggested a fellow Christian, who agreed to make all the repairs for about $800 if Howie bought the parts. Howie had to wait a few weeks for all the parts and the repairs, but he got the car back. It held together until he traded it in for his next car, a beautiful Chrysler 300 in mint condition. He managed to negotiate down the asking price this time and schmoozed the salesperson for a trade-in price of his first car for $1,000.00.

With a more trustworthy car for long-distance driving, Howard announced he wanted to take a road trip to Oklahoma to visit his birth mother. Deb told me the two of them had been talking about this for a few weeks. His explanation went something like this, "I need to go there and see if I am going to start a relationship or end one." I knew if we said no, he would go anyway.

We only knew that he even made it to Oklahoma because of a Facebook picture he had been tagged in by his birth mom. The post read, "My baby boy is home!" When "Mr. Impulsive" returned two weeks later, he declared he and his two travel buddies were all moving to Oklahoma. They were all going to get jobs and live with his birth mom. On Father's Day weekend, I became fully aware of his plan. Howie decided to restart his old relationship; with his mom but end the one we had started.

With his first visit to Oklahoma, we only heard from Howie once. After moving back to Oklahoma, most phone calls were initiated by Harley. Harley simply wanted to talk to his older brother who had been such a big part of his young life. Deb and I understood his physical absence because Howie was living in another state. What we had not properly prepared Harley for was the emotional absence that would follow. Deb and I attributed this to the phenomenon we witnessed in so many sibling groups that we fostered over the years. When the older foster sibling finally relinquishes their parental duties, when they started trusting Deb and me more, they started exploring an independent life. Why would Howie be any different? Howie had been Harley's pseudo parent and protector for many years. After Howard finally trusted us to care for Harley, he just drove away.

When we finally got a mailing address, I tried to keep in touch by writing him letters.

> *Just hours before Turkey Day, waiting for the family to arrive and I wanted to send you a note. I hope all is okay and you did have a good feast with all the fixings. If for any reason you are not feeling very thankful this holiday season, I wish you would really reconsider. We know that this adulting thing that you are doing may seem difficult at times, but if you can plan for a future, perhaps some big career opportunities are just down the road. Get in your head that you are not going to settle for minimum wage, and someday you will get there. However, you may have to make some initial short-term sacrifices before it gets better. These short-term sacrifices may seem big today, but in the bigger picture, they can change depending on how you look at things now. We love you, Bud.*

Unfortunately for Howie, his birth mom asked him and his friends to move out a few weeks later. Fortunately for Howie, he had reconnected with his brothers long enough to find a house they could rent together. He was able to find a job at a local restaurant drive-in, but it took him a long time to find this job, so he stopped making his loan and car insurance payments. He ended up meeting a girl there and fell madly in love. Then, when something happened to his car, Howie left the car where it stalled out. Howie's DNA kicked in, and he did what he always witnessed growing up; he just walked away.

Fortunately for us, we eventually figured out what was wrong with the car when we hired a tow truck company to locate the car, and take it to a neighborhood mechanic, I found doing an internet search. The owner and his wife were both so kind and they helped me work with our insurance company to determine what damage had occurred to Howie's car. What Howie did not understand was that even though he had walked away from his Chrysler 300, in mint condition, we could not default on the loan because I was a co-signer. We continued to pay the car insurance because we had a loan on the vehicle, and it was required. After the insurance adjuster contacted us, he explained his best guess. The driver had hit something big; he suspected a deer. Howie finally admitted to hitting a deer and leaving the car on the side of the road. Eventually, his roommates convinced him to push the car back to the house he was renting. Howie thought it was a nuisance; he wanted to just leave the car where it was.

I do not know if Deb ever told you about her dad. He was a nice guy. A real nice guy. He was teaching me how to use a band saw once when we went to visit them. A few times, I went into his shop on my own and used his saw to cut out shapes that I would later paint. One time the saw blade broke. I was nervous. I did not know what to do. At first, I thought I would clean up the area and make it look like I had not used it, and I thought maybe if I did not say anything, he wouldn't know it was me. Instead, when he came into the shop, I told him the blade broke. He said that it was an older blade; it was probably going to happen sooner or later. So, he got out a new blade and showed me how to put it on and then showed me how to keep the blade and machine clean, so it would last longer. He also showed me how to make a series of cuts, so that the blade would not bend as much and break. I kept all those lessons with me so when I bought my own band saw, I kept it for years

and never had any issues. He was a good man.
I really miss him. I learned that telling him the
truth was better because I trusted him. I wish
you had trusted us enough to tell us the truth.

Although Howie no longer had trustworthy transportation, one of our foster children had been adopted by a lovely couple who lived in the same state. We paid the deductible and had the car repaired. Deb called the couple and asked them if they could use an extra car. It turns out our first foster daughter was now of driving age and the family was also in need of extra transportation. We paid off the loan and gifted her and her family a Chrysler 300, in somewhat mint condition. They were so grateful, and we were so delighted. For us, we were overjoyed that the car once owned by our very last foster child was now gifted to the first foster child we ever took in.

Bud, this last week we had to make a tough
decision about a car that I knew you loved. You
told me you loved it even before I asked you
which car. But, as much as we care about you,
I knew that if you had those car payments and
insurance payments looming over your head,
you might never get above water. You cannot
move forward if something is always holding
you back. So, even though you may not think
so, we did this because we care so much about
you. You might think that it is strange that two
people can say this even after only knowing you
for a short time. Perhaps, you could compare
this to the same feelings you had for your latest
girlfriends. You can see how you can care about
someone deeply after only knowing them for
a short time. That is what happened when
we met you and Harley. We are hoping that

without these big payments you can move forward. Keep Swimming. Keep swimming.

We tried to keep in contact with Howard and Harley's older sister as well. She called Harley often. Sometimes the sister would share that she had been communicating with Howard and his latest girlfriend. She shared something with us that this new girlfriend had texted to her. So, in my final letter to Howie, I informed him that I was struggling with his sister's story.

On the way to the bus stop, your older sister was trying to tell me about a text or messenger conversation she had with your current girlfriend. Apparently, your sister was trying to tell us you had told her to back off and let you live your own life. Then your girlfriend went on to say that we always try to control you from Arizona. We know your sister, but we do not know your girlfriend. We are trying to figure out why she would say this because she does not even know us. But we know you. If you felt this way you should deliver the message; not your sister, and not a girlfriend. So, we are going to let it go. Still not sure why your sister chose to tell us how you may be feeling about us. Sounds like you are trying to walk away from something else.

Angry Texts

The small Oklahoma town that Howie was staying in was rural and not densely populated. Howie and his brother lived at a couple of addresses. We learned this when he would Facetime us and saw he was living in a new place. Whenever we asked what happened to their old place, if they could not pay his rent after a month or two, the landlord would ask them to leave and they would just walk away from the rental property, leaving everything behind. After Howie was fired from his last job in this small town, we believe Howie had finally burned all his bridges. With no doors opening in Oklahoma, Howie decided to move back to Arizona. He showed up on our doorstep carrying a duffel bag. All the household items we presented him after graduation to set up his first apartment and the Christmas gifts we had just given him; he just walked away from it all. What he did manage to bring back with him was an arrogant attitude and a strong addiction to vaping and marijuana. Knowing he had tasted independence, we tried to give him a little more leniency. After a few weeks, my patience and grace were running low. How do I know this? I know this because I had not deleted my text messages to Howie. As I read through them, it was clear to me, my tone was not positive nor supportive.

March 22, 2018–Kevy: So, heard you had to be woken up to get to work. That's disappointing. Don't know if you still have a job. Hope you do. So, you owe us some money again. Let's start with the oil change I asked you to get weeks ago and you blew me off. We would like the first 30 dollars by Saturday. If you don't have enough from your Burger King check, you can start by selling that scooter to someone or returning it. May we also strongly suggest that, until we get the rest of the 350, you limit your trips to and from work. No more journeys to Avondale, Prescott, Tucson, or anyplace else until you have paid us back.

March 24, 2018–Howie: Hey, sorry, I meant to text. I stayed over at my friends for a couple of nights I didn't have much gas and his house is closer to my work. Then yesterday he showed up at Burger King when I got off and we just kind of hung out. Sorry, I will do a better job at informing you.

April 25, 2018–Kevy: Why are you still out?! Instead, you should be figuring out how you could be more rested and then show up 30 minutes early tomorrow. Try harder to keep a job.

April 26, 2018–Kevy: So why are you ignoring my texts? We thought you were going to let us know your whereabouts every 24 hrs.

April 28, 2018 – Kevy: So, I guess your phone only works when YOU want something. Tools or money to fix cars. If you decide to show your face today; let's try something you need to practice. Honesty. No excuses. No, My Bads. No Stories. No Bullshit. Just Honesty.

April 30, 2018–Kevy: So, you have a new battery in a car, but you can't drive because you lost your keys. That must really suck. You are right about one thing: your impulsive behavior does cause you constant problems. But you are wrong if you think this is about money. Did you forget that you walked away from the Chrysler 300 and left us 2,000 in damages and 5,000 in a loan and we had to pay that all off? We didn't ask you for that did we? This is more about the way you are living your life. You are stuck in the past. Whenever you decide to make a change, we will still be there to help you out when you ask. But until then, you still owe us a sincere apology face to face.

May 3, 2018–Kevy: This is Howard's family. We have not seen him or heard from him for a full week. Do you have any numbers we could try? Can you help us out?

Howard's Friend: Hello. I apologize for the late response, but I'm afraid I do not have any numbers. I don't believe he has a cell phone number at the moment. However, I did manage to contact Howard and told him about the situation.

On May 10, 2018, an officer was leaving his substation in an unmarked patrol vehicle. The officer observed a male riding a white-colored, gas-powered motor scooter eastbound in the bike lane traveling at approximately 40 miles an hour. This officer noticed the scooter was absent a headlight, a rear taillight, no facing license plate, and the rider did not have any eyewear or eye protection. The police report indicated the officer proceeded eastbound with the intent to intercept the rider on the vehicle with multiple traffic violations. The officer positioned his patrol car directly behind the rider when he stopped at a red traffic light. The driver of the vehicle then turned and waved to the officer, but remained at the stop-light after the traffic signal changed. Then, the scooter accel-erated eastbound through the intersection, at which point the officer conducted a traffic stop. Per the police report, the driver advised the officer he was driving home from a friend's house. The driver indicated he had purchased the vehicle and was informed by the previous owner he could drive the scooter in the bicycle lane without registration.

You all probably guessed by now, but when the officer asked the driver to offer up his Arizona driver's license, it was Howie. Next, the officer conducted a record check and discovered Howie did not have a motorcycle endorsement but indicated he had a bill of sale. The officer requested the documentation for the vehicle. Howie stepped off the bike and opened the vehicle storage compartment located below his seat and retrieved a bill of sale for the vehicle. The document listed a VIN number for the vehicle; however, the officer was unable to locate that VIN number for the scooter on the bill of sale.

Howie disclosed that he had a jacket in the vehicle storage compartment, but then Howie corrected his original statement and said the jacket belonged to his friend. As any observant officer would, he asked Howie if there was any contraband in the compartment. As described in the report, Howie shook his head in a negative way and stated, "Not that he knew of." Relying on his years of training and expertise, the officer suspected Howie was not being honest. After a long moment of silence passed, Howie admitted there was marijuana in the storage compartment, and he just picked up the marijuana from a friend. Howie also offered up that he did not have a medical marijuana card. As another officer arrived on the scene, Howie presented a glass jar with a "small but usable quantity of green-colored, plant-like substance consistent with marijuana." Howie was placed under arrest for violating possession of marijuana and violating the state statute by knowingly possessing a usable quantity of the plant-like substance.

We cannot say with certainty that this was the first time Howie's arms were secured behind his back and handcuffed. We can say with certainty, however, that Howie would not be honest with us about it anyway. The report stated he was photographed and fingerprinted, and then released in the morning after a night's stay because he was positive for the presence of tetrahydrocannabinol or THC.

Deb and I hoped this would have scared him straight, but it did not. In fact, after the scooter was removed from the scene by a towing company, Impulsive Howie just walked away from that mode of transportation, too. He just left the scooter at the impound lot. There have been a series of run-ins with law enforcement over the last few years. He started with speeding tickets and advanced to possession of an illegal substance. We know this because the corrective action letters keep coming to our house. Howie did not bother to change our home address on his Arizona license. The first ones arrived giving him notice that he had failed to appear on a traffic complaint. As a result, his driving privileges were suspended for 30 days. The next set of letters requested $1,530 in fines. When those fines were not paid, the balance went to $1,828.35. The next letter indicated Howie had been convicted of driving under the influence, and his driving privileges were suspended for 90 days.

A Work in Progress

I took screenshots of the court letters and messaged them to Howie. I reminded him that he should not walk away from his responsibilities and call the courts. Time to man up. We are sadly aware that Howie had seen the inside of a jail for unpaid fines. We are woefully aware that Howie has been hired and then fired from a dozen different jobs since he came into our lives in 2015. Howie has offered up his varied versions of why he was let go each time. Interestingly enough, if we go back to the comments presented by his former teachers, his pattern of dismissals mirrors similar high school issues:

1. Often takes his phone out and needs to be told to put it away.

2. Is too social. Loves to talk. He will apologize, but then he goes right back to talking.
3. Often does not listen to his supervisor. He thinks he knows what he is doing and ignores training.
4. There is nothing that gets in his way. However, he can get off task easily and sometimes has a hard time following directions or orders.

What Deb and I know is that Howie is a work in progress. We have heard from his adopted sisters, Abby, and Miranda, that Howie does not think he is worthy of our family. He thinks this gives him permission to not get close. He is so wrong. We wish Howie could trust us more and not put so much impulsive energy into walking away from us.

On February 10, 2020, Howard called us to tell us he was going to be a dad. Six months later, in August, this life-changing event gave us hope that a baby might bring about a wee bit more maturity, or a less impulsive Howie. We are anticipating, excitedly, that fatherhood could bring about a little change. What we know for certain, we will continue to show Howie we are still his family. Deb and I already love his son, Sebastian, our eighth grandchild. I have already nicknamed him "Seabiscuit," and we adore him, as much as we love Howie.

12

FINDING JOY AGAIN

M iranda and Brandon were married on a sweltering summer day in July, at his parent's farm. The day was uncomfortably hot and humid. Yet, it was a joyous time of new beginnings, as this young couple exchanged their vows surrounded by committed family members, as well as endearing life-long friends in a lush flower garden filled with the colors of lavender, ivory, and yellow. This clan of family and friends who cheerfully joined them on that July day would continue as their support system in the years ahead as they willingly walked the path of parenthood.

As we fast forward a decade, Deb and I had a front-row seat watching their young family grow as they followed in our footsteps by taking a similar track as foster and adoptive parents. Miranda and Brandon were blessed with two biological children, Kyan and Brayah. They also adopted Tayveon, Lilly, and Giovany. Rounding out the family number to five; three boys and two girls. If you are a parent, you already know the role of caregiver, supporter, encourager, and teacher can be problematic. To add to this challenge, raising children who have come from trauma and the foster care system is extremely challenging. However, like Deb and me, Miranda and Brandon felt called to provide a safe haven for all God's children.

What you rarely realize, until they arrive on your doorstep holding just a plastic shopping bag of hastily collected possessions in their tight little fists, is that little people carry a ton of baggage. A great majority also arrive with an undiscovered diagnosis. Their youngest son, for example, was later identified with Autism, just a mere month after Miranda and Brandon signed their adoption papers. Gio has extreme behaviors and often needs one-on-one supervision, as well as multiple therapies.

Gio struggles but his parents pour into him daily; guiding him, redirecting him, whispering close to his ear; until his body relaxes and he reenters back into the world we are in. Most often, Gio is a joy to be around; his quick wit always makes us laugh. Yet, often Gio's disabilities hinder him from fully functioning the way most parents would want a typical child to behave. As a result, through his ups and downs, Miranda and Brandon found it was best for their young family to work flexible jobs to deal with their children's needs and unpredictable behaviors.

Before Gio joined their family, Miranda and Brandon had also adopted their oldest son, Tayveon. In 2019, he was diagnosed with Reactive Attachment Disorder. Tayveon's impulsive actions and their family's trek through these uncharted waters have been exhausting and heartbreaking. As a child diagnosed with RAD, Tayveon has often been a danger to himself. These erratic behaviors can be so scary for a young family who did not know his analysis early on.

The first call came without warning. When I checked the screen on my phone, I saw it was Miranda, so I answered it. I could tell immediately something was wrong. In rushed words, between choking sobs, Miranda was able to tell me that something was not right with Tayveon. She had all the other kids downstairs huddled together and Tayveon, in his room, was acting strangely. He was scaring everyone. Miranda was asking – no, *begging* — for me to come to her house. Luckily, her family only lived a few minutes from us. Miranda met me at the door, "He is in his room. I can hear him throwing things around. The other kids have not seen him like this before. They are really scared!"

I assured Miranda, "I got this!" As I walked upstairs, I gave her a look that said, focus on the other kids. When I reached his bedroom door, I knocked. He did not answer, but I could hear him moving around. I tried to open the door, and immediately understood he had pushed something up against it. Miranda is a petite 5'1". She could eventually battle her way through what was blocking the door, but she had four other kids to contend with. I am a little bigger than 5'1", a little broader than my daughter, and a wee bit stronger than an eleven-year-old. I leaned against the door, the chest of drawers slid over the carpet, as I squeezed through the opening. First, I set the piece of furniture upright and moved it away from the door. Then, I turned and saw Tayveon huddled in the corner of his room, on top of his bed. I could hear mutterings; at first, I thought he was just mumbling. As I moved closer to him, I could not make out the words. Tayveon's utterances were not words anyone would recognize; I thought to myself, "is he speaking in tongues or in Klingon?"

A few images appeared in my head, one from the 1973 movie, "The Exorcist," another from an episode of Star Trek. Was I really seeing a suggestion of a person in a dreamlike state or a trance, as referenced in the bible? Knowing Tayveon was desperately seeking attention right now, then I leaned toward "attention-seeking" as opposed to speaking in tongues. Deb and I had worked with so many different foster kids by the time Tayveon had come along, I was skeptical. We had seen desperate attention-seeking behaviors before, and some were elaborately staged as Tayveon was delivering right now. If Tay had done his homework, it might have been more convincing than the gibberish he was producing at the moment. He was not thrashing about or trying to levitate off the bed, only opting to verbalize nonsense sounds.

I settled in on his bed and reassessed the situation. Would I need to do a full restraint as we had learned in foster care training or use a different approach? I knew my immediate goal was to remove Tayveon from his room. I had already told Deb before I left, "I am going to bring him back home with me. Let's give Miranda a break from his outburst." Not wanting to have the situation escalate by attempting a restraint hold, I slid closer to Tay and tried talking to him. After a few minutes, I could see, no calming words were working. He was not hurting himself, but his actions had other people worried.

I finally landed on this approach, "Really, this is the best you can come up with? Speaking in gibberish and acting out. Listen, kiddo, this is not my first rodeo or my first exorcism, so let's clean up your room, pack a bag and you can come home and hang out with me and Grandma." I waited, and waited, and waited, and reminded him I wasn't leaving his room until he was done with his little show, his room was picked up and he had a bag packed so he could spend a few days with us. Then I waited some more. Eventually, he stopped talking, and together, we cleaned up his room, and I helped him pack his bag. We met Miranda near the door on our way out, and I told her Grandma and I wanted Tay to stay at our house for a few days. The look on her face was that of relief.

At our house, Tay acted like nothing had happened. Some parents might be excited the incident was behind them; we were not. We were all worried because Tayveon showed no remorse for frightening his family. His spontaneous, self-indulgent behaviors continued to dominate his parents' time. Miranda and Brandon have been forced to make numerous concessions for their children, especially Tay before his diagnosis with RAD. They were doing what they could, wrangling in his impulsive, destructive behaviors, while trying to parent four other children, including one with Autism. A diagnosis of Reactive Attachment Disorder provides some clarity when you learn, as a young child, he never formed a secure, healthy emotional bond with his primary caretakers. Sadly, his emotional bond never happened with the adoptive parents, either. Kids like Tayveon, who suffer from RAD, know exactly which paternal buttons to push so they do not have to attach to another human being. The simple goal of Tay's misbehavior was to sustain a predictable and reliable cycle of self-imposed rejection. Most likely, Tay's behaviors were a direct result of a negligent parent or even more dangerous an inconsistent parent or care provider.

We all agreed with the medical experts, Tay's behaviors lined up with a RAD diagnosis. In our thirteen years of fostering experience, inconsistent parental caregivers — most likely intoxicated or using drugs — make no effort whatsoever to meet the needs of their children. More precariously, when biological parents are intermittently clean and sober, they come across as overly vigilant. These inconsistent doting flashes of parenthood usually lead to confusion for the children. These poor babies are duped as they get caught up in an ill-fated world of false hopes and empty promises. Basically, they build up walls, rejecting all relationships in order to survive.

After the RAD diagnosis, Miranda and I started researching this disorder. We learned, there are some clinicians who believe you must first evoke rage in children before these broken babies can have any healing breakthroughs. Purposely making Tay angry, did not seem practical or safe. What Miranda, Brandon, Deb, and I learned is that there were dozens of different methods claiming to work, claiming guaranteed success. Some radical approaches related to a treatment model known as *regressive corrective attachment therapy*, a form of rebirthing technique. In this practice, people are wrapped in blankets and pillows, while they go through a symbolic rebirth and then handed off to their attachment figure. As we researched treatments, some just came across as so bizarre. Just as bizarre as Tay's latest bouts with impulsive and erratic behaviors.

What we all came to understand is that regulating this disorder was not in our immediate wheelhouse or expertise. Tay's parents fully grasped that; they would need the help of professionals. Until professional services could be obtained, Miranda and Brandon would muster their inner courage while they weathered through Tay's impractical or impactful choices. For the longest time, especially during his preteen years, Miranda and Brandon were so diligent in monitoring his social media, his texts, his emails, his coming and going. Tay's unfathomable choices widened the rift between him and his parents. With each week, with each new incident, with each new lie; Miranda and Brandon sadly came to comprehend that in order for Tay to move forward with a successful healing, his parents would have to let him go. They would have to get him into an intensive treatment center and soon.

One of the most disturbing behaviors for his family was his stealing. Not just from strangers or his classmates at school, but his own family. Tay's immediate need for self-gratification was hard to explain away or justify the stealing of his sister's, a brother's, or parent's possessions. Their things, and subsequent disappointment, were merely collateral damage and not his major concern. Tayveon simply shrugged off the visible displeasure on his father's face, even after admitting he had helped himself to his dad's coin collection to feed a school vending machine for a sugar fix. Nothing would faze him. Yet, his mom and dad never stopped trying. With every incident, Tay's deep desire for self-indulgence was met by a parent lecture or a consequence. His impulses continued to heighten, until one day. Tay broke his hand after punching a few holes in his bedroom walls. His erratic and self-injurious behaviors had crested. Miranda and Brandon had to make the toughest decision for a parent; they took him to the Emergency Room knowing there would be consequences. Tay had truly become a danger to himself and would be hospitalized for five weeks with intensive therapy.

My first visit to see Tay became a grim reality when the attendants took away the gifts I thought I could give to our grandson. In a mental health facility, they explained, "your grandson may hurt himself with the sharpened drawing pencils or the wire spiral of the sketchbook." As the trusted professionals, they shrugged and said I would get the gifts back when I signed out. With no other gifts in hand, we were left with a single deck of playing cards while we tried to talk about his therapy. Brandon and I sat with him in a bare hallway on plastic chairs attempting a card game. We were not allowed in a patient's room; they needed to keep their eyes on him at all times. Together, we passed the assigned hour staring at each other, holding our cards, making small talk, glancing at other families, similarly clustered together experiencing the same gut-wrenching circumstances. The experience was sterile; it was awkward; it was a discouraging reality.

While Tay was away, Miranda and Brandon desperately tried to keep their family functioning as normally as they could; with one child in a mental health facility, one with autism, and the rest of their crew muddling through. They were quickly learning the ins and outs of insurance coverage, lengths of stay allowed, and all that occurs with this type of medical treatment.

Brayah, already in the school choir, was scheduled to sing the national anthem at an Arizona Diamondbacks game. Her parents were determined some things should stay normal and move ahead as planned. Brayah and Brandon would go, enjoy her performance, and even stay for the game. At the time Miranda and Brandon made this decision, Tayveon was still in the facility.

On the day of the game and performance, the family received word Tayveon was being released. The facility determined Tayveon had not attempted any self-harming behaviors in several days, so he was no longer considered a threat to himself. When Miranda told me this, I could see the worry in her eyes. I knew where I was needed. As soon as I got home from work, I headed over to their house to hang out until Brandon and Brayah returned from the Diamondbacks game. That was our plan, but sometimes well-intended plans do not always go the way we hope.

Brandon has always been careful about monitoring the older boys and their video time. Like other hands-on parents, he uses parental controls to limit their times. If either of the older boys wanted to increase their playing time, Tayveon or Kyan would have to talk to Brandon and negotiate for extended minutes. In most situations, Brandon always had the final say. The older boys knew this. Within minutes after Brandon and Brayah left for the Diamondback games, Tayveon challenged Miranda about adding more playing time. Even though Tayveon was pressuring her, telling Miranda he needed the time to calm himself down, Miranda stayed firm. Tay would have to talk to his dad to increase his playing time, not her.

Tayveon knew his dad was at a baseball game and would not be home for several hours. The chance of him answering a phone call or a text request would be slim to none. I am certain Tayveon knew exactly what he was doing when he asked his Mom for more playing time. He was purposely trying to intimidate and manipulate Miranda by using his own diagnosis and recent medical stay to get what he wanted. He had just been released from a mental health facility and in his myopic mind, he deserved more time. When Miranda told him not yet, he heard, "NO!" and decided to finesse the situation in his favor.

His first action, Tayveon unwrapped the hand he had fractured after putting his fist through the wall. I discovered this when I went into his room to check on him after I arrived at

Miranda's. Miranda was already upset, and she had every right to feel that way.

I knew Tayveon had previously cracked some bones in his hand after he fist pounded the wall. When I suggested unwrapping his hand might cause more damage, he just started thumping his fist on the top of his desk. It was intentional, but not strong enough to do more damage at this point. I left him to go and report what I had seen to Miranda and came back to the second act of Tayveon's manipulation. He had wrapped himself in a blanket and moved to a corner of his room. I grabbed his chair by his desk and propped myself in front of him so I could study his physical reactions or his face as I spoke to him. Yet, no matter what I said to him, he refused to talk.

I was attempting different topics, asking probing questions, seeking out any reaction from him. I was trying to see if I could break through this self-imposed trance, this haze that was overshadowing him. When I started asking questions about the drawings and writings on his wall, I hit a nerve. Tayveon started thumping his fractured hand against the wall with purpose. I knew he was no longer in the right state of mind. I would not attempt a restraint if he had made the decision to hurt himself again.

As the father of seven, and a foster dad of many, I understood, most kids who wanted things to go in their favor, would stop their rants or tantrums and try to negotiate with me. If the desired goal was to change the mind of this parent, then use your personal attachment to manipulate my emotions. However, with Tayveon, a child diagnosed with RAD, he was not interested in developing or even accepting a relationship. In his mind, when he wanted something, nothing was going to get in his way. Nothing, including the act of hurting himself.

I kept thinking, that if I could get through to him and just get him to talk to me; I could make him stop. When I went back into his room, I took a closer look at the drawings and the writings. I saw several places where Tayveon had been scribbling on the walls, in his closet, on his desk, and his bed frame. I learned later; he had even written on the blades of his ceiling fan. Some of the words spoke of the desire to go deeper with his faith; a yearning to have a closer relationship with God. Thinking this might be an open door, I tried to interject God's promises reminding him, he was not alone. He had his siblings, parents, grandparents, and most importantly, God. God loved him and God did not want him to feel alone. After a few minutes, I realized no verses or scripture were making an impact. In fact, his thumping on the wall was getting louder and stronger.

I truly felt I had seen enough. I went back out into the living room and told Miranda how his behaviors were escalating. I could not see an easy solution to this. In my mind, I did not think Tayveon should have been released. I had strong feelings after watching him for the last half hour. I could see he was still manipulating the situation and he was still self-injurious. I stepped in closer, wrapped my arms around my daughter, and told her, "You need to call the police. You cannot do this alone. You need their guidance and help. He cannot stay here. He is not safe. He needs to go back to the hospital. He has only been home for 45 minutes. Tayveon made his choice, now you will have to make one, too."

Within minutes, I was opening the door for an officer from the Maricopa Sheriff's Department. As he walked by me, I could see his utility belt, and my eyes were drawn to his sidearm. I could see the ambulance and the first responders pulling up to the house. Here we go again. This was all so surreal. I walked the police officer to his bedroom and I immediately saw Tayveon sitting on his chair, at his desk, with his back to the doorway. He had left the corner of the room, thrown his blanket back on bed, and was finishing rewrapping his hand.

As soon as I saw all this, I knew Tay had manipulated the whole scene. Tay was showing the officer he was not in any distress or hurting himself. The police officer stood above him as he tried talking to Tayveon. He began by asking him general questions; his name, his age, what year in school he was. Tayveon looked down at his hand and would not say a word. The officer and I were receiving the same silent treatment. Because Tayveon was not talking, the officer started looking around the room and noticed the writings and images on the walls, the bed frame, and he even looked inside the closet. Next, he noticed the places where Tay had punched the holes in the wall. He started to connect all the dots as he moved his gaze over to Tay's bandaged hand. The officer leaned into Tayveon and asked him if he felt like he wanted to hurt himself or did he want to hurt anyone else.

That was when Tayveon turned on the waterworks and huge crocodile tears ran down his cheeks. I felt these were real; I was overwhelmed with sadness. Tayveon had experienced weeks without his family, undergone emergency room visits, endured therapy sessions, with little or no progress. At this moment, I think Tayveon knew himself, he was not ready to come home either. He did not have his emotions or his rage under control.

I heard Miranda talking to the paramedics in the other room, and they were moving into the room with Tayveon, the officer, and me. With so many people in his bedroom, I moved to the kitchen. One of the first responders checked his hand, with the officer close by. The other two talked with Miranda for a few more minutes. Together as a team, they made the decision to take Tayveon to an emergency room and request a psych consult. The paramedics put Tayveon on a gurney and strapped him down, wheeling him out of his room, past Miranda and I, and out the door to the ambulance. After Miranda found out what hospital they were taking Tayveon to, we left her kids with Abby, and grabbed a few things, and drove to the hospital.

By the time we reached the emergency room, the staff had Tayveon out of his street clothes and into some scrubs.

He was in a room, behind a sliding glass door. Except for a bed, a small rolling table, and a chair, there was little else in the room. While we waited for a doctor to see him, Miranda and I were given two chairs to sit in the hallway, next to a young man whose sole job was to observe Tayveon. As we chatted, Miranda and I watched Tayveon pacing back and forth. He was falling into a routine where he would stop pacing, get up on the bed, and cover himself with a sheet. A few minutes later, he would uncover himself, get off the bed, and then start pacing back and forth again. It was like watching a caged animal as we sat and stared at him through the glass doors.

After hours had passed, a staff member told Miranda a doctor was ready to talk to them as a tv monitor came to life. Miranda walked through the sliding glass door and began to answer some questions for the virtual meeting with the psychologist. Tayveon was quiet as he laid on the bed, wrapped in the sheet, listening to both the psychiatrist and his mother talking about what had transpired at the house. After Miranda finished her time, she stepped out, and now it was Tayveon's turn to talk to the tv monitor.

Before this emergency room visit, Tayveon had just spent several weeks in a mental health facility. He had endured several conversations with therapists and psychiatrists. He had listened to their interrogations and learned how he answered their questions would determine if the sessions would go by quickly or last longer. Even though their conversation was muffled through the glass doors, I saw how Tayveon had come off the bed, left the sheet behind him, and stood in front of the monitor; blocking the face of the psychologist. He was no longer pacing back and forth or cowering under the sheet. In my gut, I felt Tayveon was manipulating this conversation, just as he had tried to manipulate his mother only a few hours ago. Tayveon was up close and personal, studying her questions, watching her reactions. My gut was saying, this boy is desperately trying to get himself out of this situation.

I suggested to Miranda that she and I step away for a few minutes. The conversation with the psychologist was supposed to be private, and the young man was still monitoring Tayveon from the hallway. We found a quiet corner and discussed our interpretation and possible results of the consultation. We both felt strongly that the psychologist would be recommending a release to the attending doctor. I could see Miranda was extremely overwhelmed.

As we were walking back to Tay's room, we passed the nurse's station where the attending doctor was sitting at a desk. Miranda quickened her pace and walked up to the counter, looking right into the eyes of the doctor, "What happens next?" The doctor informed her that he was waiting for a call back from the psychologist with her recommendations. He started to explain to Miranda, if the psychologist agreed Tayveon was non-injurious, he would be released. Just hearing the doctor say the word "release" caused a flood of emotions. All her anxieties and worries came rushing out in a mash-up of words and tears. Miranda told the doctor about Tay's RAD diagnosis, his broken hand, the holes in the walls, the suicidal ideations, and the fear of what would happen if Tayveon came home without a treatment plan in place. I was close enough to watch the doctor's face and I could see it change from all business to a look of compassion and sadness. Then the phone in front of him rang, he looked at Miranda and said, "I need to take this." Miranda, stepped back, put her hands over her face, sobbing as she walked away from the nurse's station. My daughter was exhausted.

A few minutes later, the doctor came to the area where Miranda and I had been sitting. He stood above her and calmly said, "Miranda, we are admitting him, Tayveon will not be going home with you today."

After she signed the paperwork, she went into the room to talk to Tayveon. He did not react when Miranda tried to say goodbye. He had not convinced the doctors; he had not been able to manipulate his way out this time. I was relieved Tayveon was not coming home with us, but watching my grandson slipping away mentally, was disheartening. I felt so helpless. With her signature, Miranda had been given the gift of time for Tayveon. Another thirty days of treatment, perhaps more. More time with people who were schooled and trained to help break down the walls of an attachment disorder. This doctor, who saw the pain in her eyes and heard her plea, had given my daughter hope.

After his recent actions, Miranda and Brandon learned Tayveon would be moving into a behavioral group home for five months. During those five months, his new team would be focused on treating several areas, including: aggression, depression, anxiety, sleep disturbances, ADHD, PTSD, and so much more. The group home's primary goal was to bring about emotional regulation while aiding Tay in acknowledging his behaviors, as well as making him accountable for his prior and ongoing actions.

If you are asking yourself, "how could a parent hand over their child to a home filled with strangers?" The answer is not simple, it is not easy. How could you walk away and leave him there, not knowing what you would find the next time you visit? Deb and I can attest from our own experience with Abby, the act of letting go is so hard. It is damn, hard. We knew deep in our souls; this act of release would be just as difficult for Miranda and Brandon.

I can still recall the night Deb and I drove away from the group home where we left Abby in rehab. As we sat in our car before we pulled away from the curb, I turned to Deb and said, "What in the hell did we just do?" What we did was give Abby to God and trusted in our Lord to watch over her in our absence. Miranda and Brandon would have to keep the faith and do the exact same thing for Tayveon.

You must have faith. You must believe the decision you make to save your child's life is the right thing to do. This action of release and letting go is the only thing you can do to make your family whole again. For Miranda and Brandon, and, for Deb and me, we predicted it would be a complicated, emotionally taxing journey. A journey we both feared at the time would have a negative impact on our children. Yet, through these journeys, we both taught their siblings that sometimes when their actions come across as being hurtful, it is because the individual is hurting inside even more.

Each of our children has learned through faith how to handle extreme behaviors and all different types of trauma. By doing what Jesus would do, we can show our children grace, and love. We have been through some hard times! Yet, through pain and heartache, we have seen God work wonders in our world. We have experienced a peace that surpasses all understanding.

Most times, our families arrive at a place where we feel whole again. When this happens, we give all the glory to GOD! Through the years there have been struggles. What we know, God has been faithful walking alongside us. Sometimes he has even picked us up and carried us.

Miranda's middle namesake was gifted from my mom, Marilyn Joyce Sieling. Miranda was the first of our seven. Her birth brought us Joy. A Joy I never thought I would be able to experience because I was so afraid the sins of my father would be passed down to me. Yet, I found Joy, again. Through her faith, Miranda has given her son Tayveon to God, and she will find Joy again.

After Tayveon's stay in the group home, his arrival at home was met with tremendous anxiety. Did all the hard work of the group home stick with him? The first few days were filled with apprehension. We all kept waiting for that proverbial shoe to drop, but it really has not. As a family, parents and son are still working through doing life together. Doing life through a pandemic has proved to be both a challenge and a bonus. Their close quarters have forced them all to do more listening and less lecturing. There have been numerous heartfelt reflections of Tay's previous actions towards his parents and his siblings. There have been innumerable honest and meaningful conversations on how God has impacted all of them through this Joyful journey. On Mother's Day, 2020, Miranda received this note from Tayveon.

> *Mom,*
>
> *This past year has been rough. But I will just say, while I was in the group home, I would look forward to seeing you and hearing your laugh. What I always knew, you loved me. It was hard at first, but I knew it would be alright. You were always going to be there. I regret the times I told you I did not want you there. I regret that. I do not ever remember saying sorry. I am so sorry. I am saying it now. I am sorry.*
>
> *Love Tayveon*

A true prodigal can almost always bring you Joy. Yet, sometimes simple Joy can be found in other measures.

The Joy of Cleaning

For example, an extremely personal Joy for me came after I moved into my first apartment in Moorhead. Before my purest of pleasures evolved, I had to reach back in time and identify a set of vivid memories; those recollections of living with a set of parents who loved or needed to collect stuff. I think it was dad more than mom, but it could have been both of them. The kitchen counters were always cluttered, every drawer was a junk drawer. As a preteen, I slept in the basement in a room with two twin beds and no door. My older brothers slept in another room with two double beds and a door that worked. There was a working toilet and a sink, but once again, there was no door for the makeshift bathroom in the basement. There was no light switch in the basement. The on-off switch was at the top of the stairs. You either had one person go down the stairs to the bedroom first to turn on a ceiling light in your room, or you would carefully swing your arms back and forth, feeling your way until you reached your room. If you kept the light off, you had to be careful not to trip on anything on the stairs because it was filled with old shoes and work boots. My older brothers could reach the one light bulb in the middle of the room, so they would just unscrew the bulb once they were in their rooms. They had earned the right to not go back up the stairs and turn off the switch. Eventually, someone in the family installed a pull string light eliminating the need to go up and down the stairs to turn off the light. After we all went to bed, you only had to swing one arm until you hit the string. Looking back, rooms without doors, one light switch, only one way in or out; it was not a safe place for a boy's barracks.

At first, I did not realize how much my dad collected and kept stuff on the farm. After our barn burnt down, a huge pole shed was erected quickly in its place. I cannot forget, the shed was always filled with stuff. Being in real estate, my dad loved to go to auctions and bring back boxes and boxes of what others might just call junk. Perhaps he was always hoping to find that one item that might bring him riches from a pauper's purchase. He made many acquisitions to fill that pole shed. I am not sure he and mom ever threw anything away. My memories are of the garage, the basement, the pole shed, the attic space, or any nook and cranny always filled with discarded treasures. For years, I felt surrounded by other people's abandoned possessions. More stuff kept coming in and rarely left the farm. Most likely, to say we cleaned meant we moved items from one place to another place. The farm and the residence never felt clean and tidy. In addition, I do not really recall ever being taught how to deep clean a room. I know I became an expert at sweeping floors, as well as rearranging and restacking their boxes of treasures.

When I finally had my own space, there was something gratifying about clear counters with nothing on them but a toaster and a coffee pot. To sit in a living room with matching furniture and only one working television was satisfying. Best of all, to scan a room and see the fresh tracks of a recently vacuumed floor could make me misty-eyed. My life on the farm always felt messy, so cleaning my spaces has been therapeutic for me. Being surrounded by organization without clutter makes me feel as if I am in control and provides me peace. One of my favorite rituals was to make all the beds, empty laundry baskets, clean off counters, and vacuum or sweep all the floors before leaving on a vacation. My daughter confided in me one day, she never really understood why I scoured, scrubbed, dusted, and vacuumed our house from top to bottom before we left. I can still recall my kids complaining from the car for me to hurry up while I wrapped up the cord of the vacuum and stored it in the closet. My daughter said, "I didn't get it until I tried it once and experienced the pure pleasure of a squeaky-clean house after coming home from a fun-filled, but exhausting family trip." I find Joy in all this. My obsession may drive my family nuts from time to time, but a passion for cleanliness brings me bliss.

Whenever our God puts you in a situation, you immediately think that life would be so much easier and would make better sense, if all things would just go the way you want them to. I may have wanted to grow up in a picture-perfect home, but more often than not, God has a different plan. But you tell God, "My plan is not the same; I think my plan is better." God will wait and wait for you to give up on your plan, as you learn to trust Him. You are just kidding yourself by thinking you will be a better person, a better Christian if I do not have to deal with issues, troubles, or problems. Do not be the guy who gives up because life is hard. Turn your trials into triumphs and bring honor to your family and, more importantly, to Christ the King.

Even if more Sielings come crashing down in my lifetime, my children and I have experienced a God, who in His time, will continue to show us Joy again.

Joy, we have learned is different than happiness. Happiness is fleeting. Joy happens despite your circumstances. Joy is a deep-rooted spiritual sensation of hope and inspiration. Seek out Joy. If you do, as His word promises, you will find Joy again.

James 1:2-4 New Testament for Everyone

[2] My dear family, when you find yourselves tumbling into various trials and tribulations, learn to look at it with complete joy, [3] because you know that, when your faith is put to the test, what comes out is patience. [4] What is more, you must let patience have its complete effect, so that you may be complete and whole, not falling short in anything.

LIFE IS A GIFT

In the Winter of 2018, I wrote each of my seven children a personal letter and gave it to them at Christmas. To create these letters, I spoke with each of my children and asked them to tell me the qualities they admire in each other. To capture their personal reflections was my gift.

Letters to Miranda and Brandon

Miranda,

You are so creative; you have a servant heart, and You are loved. Your Mom and your Dad love the prayer warrior that you have become. We know that you always put your family first but wish you would find more time for yourself. Your brothers and your sisters love the parties and get-togethers you put together and have no idea how much time you dedicate preparing for them.

Brandon,

Our eighth child, our fifth son, oh how we adore you. You are meticulous, you are thoughtful, and you have opened your heart to several of God's children, and you are loved. Your in-laws love how much you cherish our daughter. Your brothers and sisters love that we take full advantage of the fact that you make T-shirts for a living. Your five children love that you know the importance of date night and why it must happen. Your niece and nephew love knowing your home is a safe harbor.

We said it before, but it so true. We thank God every day that you fell in love with our daughter at a Dairy Queen, and He gave you to all of us.

Mom & Dad

Letters to Danielle & Evan

Danielle,

> *Thank you for the love you give,*
> *Your love for Evan touches our hearts.*
> *Whenever we think of family,*
> *We realize you are a special part.*
> *Evan has chosen you to be,*
> *His partner and boyfriend for life,*
> *We would like you to know,*
> *We are so grateful you are his wife.*

Evan,

> *A man stands now where my baby boy once toddled,*
> *The sight of him all grown up moves me.*
> *My son has become a wiser, stronger man,*
> *More than we ever dreamed he could be.*
> *I know by looking at him that God has blessed him*
> *As an adult in the world of work and life,*
> *In my heart and soul, we love and adore our first son.*

Mom & Dad

A Letter to Abby

As an adult, we want to remind you that you are loved. Your Mom & your Dad love you. Your brothers and sisters love you and are so thankful you are actively a part of our lives again. Your nieces, nephews, and children, with all their big personalities, adore you. Most importantly, God loves you. When we look at you, we see our past, present, and future. We see our little girl growing up, wishing for brand-name clothes and makeup. We see you working in the Rothsay garden, picking flowers and vegies, and sharing them with Mom. We see a beautiful smile on your face and recognize that moment of joy you feel as a parent. No matter how old you are, you will always be our baby girl. We are so proud of you and we continue to love you with all our hearts, for all eternity.

Mom & Dad

A Letter to Stefy

Dearest Sweet Stefy,

You are so silly and sweet, as you bounce through life, and You are loved. Your Mom, Dad & your caregivers and teachers love your moments of independence. Your brothers and sisters know that you love routines and structure and try to accommodate you. Your friends and teachers at school, love you deeply. Most importantly, God loves you.

Mom & Dad

A Letter to Eddie

Dear Ed,

You are so musical; God has given you a beautiful voice and You are loved. Your Grandma loved you. Your Mom and your Dad love that you can be cuddly and will still sit on our laps. Your big brothers and sisters know that you like order and will help you when change makes you anxious or sad. Your nieces, nephews, brothers, and sisters love you (even though they must hold their ears sometimes). Your friends, teachers, and principal at school, love you.

Most importantly, God loves you. He loves how kind and caring you can be when you are not mad at Harley or Garrett. After all, He made you. He understands all the gifts you have been blessed with. Remember, there is no one else in the world like you. No one has the same gift of perfect pitch, the ability to dance with abandon or a love for pizza, as you. No one can be you, as well as you. You are a gift. Our lives would not be complete without you. We thank God every day that He chose all of us to become a family.

Mom & Dad

A Letter to Harley

Dearest Harley,

You are so goofy; you ask so many questions and You are loved. Your Grandma loved you. Your mom and your dad, who chose you, love your silliness and all your Green, Green Days. Your brothers think you are so imaginative, and your sisters think you are so loveable. Your nieces and nephews love you (even though you do not admit when you have done something wrong.) Your van drivers and teachers Love you.

Most importantly, God loves you. After all, He made you. He loves how you finally trusted your new mom and dad to take care of you. He understands when you need help doing things, we all take for granted. Always remember to be yourself. There is no one else in the world like you. No one exactly with the same fear of bugs, a big imagination, likes and dislikes, or have as many, many questions as you. You are a gift. Our lives would not be complete without you. We thank God every day that He chose us and gave us, Harley.

Mom & Dad

A Letter to Howard

Oh Howard,

The last time we were all together as a family, we asked your adopted brothers and sisters to give us words to describe you. We wanted you to know that even though we have not known you all the days of your life, when we chose you on that one important day, we made a purposeful decision to love you for the rest of your time on earth.

Because of the life you once led, we recognize that there have been some painful gaps, but we have done our best to fill them in. At times, you were both a brother and father to Harley, and we will never, ever forget that. He loves you in his own special way. As your mom and dad, even though you call us Deb and Kevy, we love you. Your brothers and sisters love you and recognize that as you continue to find your way, they will have your back if you let them. Your nieces and nephews adore you. You cannot forget they look up to you, so make them proud, and teach them what is right. Never, never, never, give up.

Mom & Dad

Dearest Tayveon,

You are so curious. You are watchfully intuitive, and You are loved. Your Grandmas and Grandpas love you. Your mom and your dad, who chose you, love that you are sensitive to animals. Your uncles think you are so adventurous, and your aunties think you can be a bit mischievous and antagonistic, a work in progress. Your little brothers and sisters love you (even though you blame them for things you do). Your church loves you.

Most importantly, God loves you. He loves how helpful you are. After all, He made you. He understands that you think you do not have to be honest, but that is not correct. Always remember to be yourself or a better version of yourself. You are a gift. Our lives would not be complete without you. We thank God every day that your mom and dad chose you and He gave us You.

As your grandparents, we are asking that you do not let others define you. People will say and do mean things. They will want you to be like them. They will try to take away your self-confidence. Do not let them. Be who God created you to be, not who someone else tells you to be.

Most of the time, the easy road is one that follows the crowd. Be wary, it may be the wrong path. Be strong and *courageous like your aunt Abby. Do not be afraid to choose the right things, even when your friends are choosing the wrong ones. Stand up for what is right, even when it is hard.*

Grandma & Grandpa

ABOUT THE AUTHOR

Kevin Sieling was born and raised in the Midwest and attended colleges in Minnesota and North Dakota. He currently resides in Arizona with his wife, Deb, three of their adopted children and their newest addition, a family dog named Bear.

CPSIA information can be obtained
at www.ICGtesting.com
Printed in the USA
LVHW030752291220
675307LV00005B/208

9 780578 766102